Spiritual birthday:
December 30, 2008

Dear ▮▮▮▮▮,

I ran across this little pink book and thought of you. Thank you for allowing me to be a part of your Spiritual birthday! You are in my thoughts + prayers each day. Learn as much as you can about your Savoir - you are in HIS thoughts each day too!   Love, Cindy

every teen girl's little pink book

special gift edition

by Cathy Bartel

Harrison House
Tulsa, Oklahoma

10 09 08   10 9 8 7 6 5 4

every teen girl's little pink book special gift edition
ISBN 13: 978-1-57794-909-1
ISBN 10: 1-57794-909-9
Copyright © 2007 by Cathy Bartel
P.O. Box 691923
Tulsa, Oklahoma 74179

Published by **Harrison House, Inc.**
P.O. Box 35035
Tulsa, Oklahoma 74153

contents

every teen girl's
little pink book

introduction

Dear friend,

Although you and I may not have ever met, I feel very honored to have this opportunity to remind you of something so amazing: *You are God's daughter!* Now, if you're unsure of that, I pray that this book will help you to know whom you belong to. God, your heavenly Father, created you with a heart that longs to be in a relationship with Him.

Think about this for a moment: God, the One who created the whole universe, formed you in your mother's womb and called you to be His daughter. How important does that make you feel? You are the daughter of the King of kings and Lord of lords! You could be called a princess! I know it makes me want to hold my head up so high, and at the same time bow down in humility!

One day when I was praying, the Lord reminded me that if I would make my relationship with Him the most important one—spending time with Him in prayer, studying His Word, and worshipping

Him—then He would help me do well in all the other things He has called me to do.

Now, take a look at this list of roles you may have as a young woman: daughter to your heavenly Father, daughter to your earthly parents, sister, granddaughter, niece, cousin, friend, best friend, student, teenager, babysitter, cheerleader, athlete, etc. As time goes on, you will gain new roles, such as employee, employer, aunt, girlfriend, fiancé, wife, daughter-in-law, sister-in-law, mother, mother-in-law, grandma, great-grandma. Oh my! As women, we wear a lot of hats.

Just remember: You don't have to wear all these hats at once. Thank goodness! I'm so thankful there are seasons in life, and the Lord prepares and equips us to take on all of these responsibilities as they come.

I am so thrilled for you to get to be a young woman in the times we are living in. He has called you for such a time as this. Trust your heavenly Father. He loved you so much that He gave His only Son, Jesus, so that if you believe in Him you will not perish but have everlasting life. You were bought with a great price! God gave His Son for you so you could be His daughter!

Have you ever seen the show *Trading Spaces*? Well, Jesus completely traded spaces with you—and not just for two days, but forever! He makes an eternal, forever, and always trade with you when you give your whole heart to Him. Some people call it The Great Exchange.

We give Him:	He gives us:
Our failures	His new beginnings
Our weaknesses	His strength
Our sadness	His joy
Our problems	His solutions
Our broken hearts	His comfort
Our pain	His healing
The impossible	"All things are possible"
Our dreams	His fulfillment
Our gifts and talents	His grace

I pray that this book will encourage you and help you to see how good God is and how precious you are to Him. I love you and want to see you grow more in love with God every day and be delighted to be His daughter!

Love,
Cathy

de-light

*to take great pleasure to give keen enjoyment; to give joy or satisfaction to*¹

Psalm 37:4 NIV says, "Delight yourself in the Lord and he will give you the desires of your heart." What do you think about that? I have to tell you, this Scripture is so dear to my heart! When I was a teenager I realized that if I would want to please the Lord in everything, He would not only give me the desires of my heart but would actually place His desires for me in my heart—and make them come true!

How amazing is that? Because you love God as your Father and because He loves you as His daughter, your desires and His desires for you become one desire! Remember: He has the absolute best plan for you.

You may be thinking, *How will I know it's God's desires I am following?* His Word and His will for you will agree. If you are delighting in the Lord, you'll be reading His Word. And if you're reading His Word, He will reveal His will to you.

Even though I haven't met you, I know you want to grow in your relationship with the Lord. Why else would you be reading this book? (By the way, I'd like to thank you. I'm very honored that you are sharing this time with me.)

As you grow in your relationship with God, you may wonder how else you can "delight yourself in the Lord."

Well, how do you take delight in your friends? You spend time with them. You talk with them, and you listen to them. Spending time with your heavenly Father is the best way to delight in Him, too. Here are a few ways you can spend time with Him:

Read the Bible. The Bible contains love letters to you from God.

Talk to Him. Listen to what God has to say to you, and tell Him how much you love Him.

Spend time with others who know Him. Go to church and Bible studies, read books like this, and listen to teaching CDs.

Every Teen Girl's Little Pink Book

Worship. Take time to tell God how much you appreciate all the good things He does for you.

Shortly after I asked Jesus to live in my heart, at around 14 years old, I was at church while an evangelist was speaking. For some reason, I looked over at his wife and thought, *I want to be a preacher's wife.* I admired her! Now, previous to that, the desire of my heart was to grow up and become a wife and a mother. Now I wanted so much to be a *preacher's* wife and a mother.

At that time, and throughout high school, I had a friend who was very annoying and would tease me to tears. I never would have imagined that he would become my husband. I had no idea if he would even have anything to do with becoming a Christian, let alone preaching the Gospel.

To make a long story short, he called me up about a year after we graduated and asked if I would like to be on a children's ministry team with him. He had been away at Bible school for a year and had learned a lot about ministering to kids with puppets and drama. My first thought was *I'll have to see this to believe it.* Well, to my surprise, he was serious—and the more I was around him, the more I literally fell in love with him. Here was a young man who loved God with all of his heart!

The desire the Lord had put in my heart several years before began to unfold right before my eyes. Blaine asked me to marry him, and for the last 25 years I have been so blessed to be at his side while he's preached to thousands of children, teenagers, and adults. Not only that, but for the last 21 years I've been busy fulfilling my dream of being a mom to three wonderful sons. I'm so thankful I delighted in the Lord and continue to do so! I know you will be thankful as you delight in the Lord, too!

Remember that God delights in you and is thinking of you right now.

> The Lord your God is with you…He will take great delight in you, He will quiet you with his love, He will rejoice over you with signing.
>
> *Zephaniah 3:17 NIV*

think pink

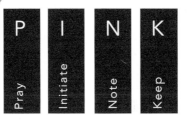

P - Pray
I - Initiate
N - Note
K - Keep

Lord, I thank You that as I delight myself in You, You give me the desires of my heart. Thank You for putting Your desires for me in my heart. Thank You for Your Word. As I study it, You write it on my heart. I hear Your voice; You are a good Father and a stranger's voice I do not follow.

de-light

You said in Your Word that You rejoice over me with singing. You calm me with Your love. You are my Savior and my Lord. I delight to do Your will, and I want to please You with all my heart. I look to Your Word because it is a lamp unto my feet and a light unto my path.

"To a father growing old, nothing is dearer than a daughter."

—Euripides[ii]

if God had a refrigerator

If God had a refrigerator,
   your picture would be on it.

If He had a wallet, your photo
   would be in it.

He sends you flowers every spring
   and a sunrise every morning.

Whenever you want to talk,
   He'll listen.

He can live anywhere in
   the universe, and
   He chose your heart.

What about the Christmas
gift He sent you in
Bethlehem, not to mention
that Friday at Calvary?

Face it, friend. He's crazy
about you.

—Author Unknown

as-pire

to seek to attain or accomplish a particular goal

ascend, soar[iii]

What a wonderful thing to be able to say as a young woman, "Imitate me as I imitate Jesus"! Paul was able to say this (1 Cor. 11:1), and we should all be on our way to saying it, if we can't say it yet.

I believe we can admire others. It's nice to look up to people and think they're something special, but let's take it a step further and aspire to be like those people in our lives whom we admire. I'm not talking about people who look like they are successful but whose lives are falling apart behind closed doors. I want you to think about those people in your life who are tried and true. They are the real thing. Nobody's perfect, but it's good to admire the people in your life who genuinely show the love of God to others.

Because we're talking about God's daughters, I want you to think of older women you want to be like. (I know you can think of at least one.) It might be your very own mom, a big sister, an aunt, a teacher, a pastor's wife, or a friend. There are people in our lives who challenge us to grow up, to do better and try harder, to be more disciplined, to love more, to smile, to love ourselves, to help others, to be more like Jesus. Just being around them, we know they have spent time with the Lord. They share His joy and compassion. If you don't know someone like that, I pray right now for God to put a godly woman like that in your life. I believe that you'll know the blessing of this kind of relationship very soon, because it is so important.

It's also important that you be someone others look up to. Your example (good or bad) will speak louder than anything you say. You need to be that person whom others look up to when they are down. Be the girl at school, church, or even the mall who inspires some little girl to say to herself, "I want to be just like her." It will thrill your heart to hear someone say, "I've been watching you, and there is something you have that I don't. What is it?" Guess what? You are a witness of the love of Christ. You are an ambassador. You are God's daughter—a daughter of not just *a* king but of *the King of kings.*

Being a Christian is not always easy. You will sometimes have to make choices that are opposite of the average teenager's. However, may I remind you, you are not average! Every time you choose to obey God's Word (your Father's letters to you), He will give you strength to conquer temptations. Others will be watching you, longing for the stability, wisdom, and strength that you demonstrate as God's daughter.

Remember: Aspire to be like someone great, and be someone others aspire to be!

think pink

P — Pray
I — .Initiate
N — Note
K — Keep

1 CORINTHIANS

11:1 AMP

Pattern yourselves after me [follow my example], as I imitate and follow Christ (the Messiah).

You are daughters of God. If each one of you could only have a sure knowledge of this for yourself, you would have a sweet peace in your heart and confidence to meet any challenges life may bring.

Jayne B. Malin[iv]

7 questions to ask your parents in the next 7 days

Asking questions is a great way to learn and grow. When you ask others about yourself, you gain a perspective on areas of your life that you may have never realized. Here are 7 questions to ask your parents in the next 7 days. Write down their answers. Then look closely, and learn as you read each one.

 How can I be a better daughter?

 What do you see as my greatest strengths?

 What do you think are the weaknesses that I must work on?

 Which friends do you see as the best influences in my life?

What kind of career could you see me getting into after I graduate?

 When do I make you most proud?

 What is the most important thing you've learned in life?

un-a-shamed

not ashamed

being without guilt, self-consciousness, or doubt"

Psalm 3:2-4 brings so much comfort to me. I pray as you read it, you'll understand how much your heavenly Father wants for you to walk upright, knowing you are right with Him.

> Many are saying of me "There is no help for him in God." But You, O Lord, are a covering around me, my shining-greatness, and the One Who lifts my head. I was crying to the Lord with my voice. And He answered me from His holy mountain.

Psalm 3:2-4 NLV

I can just see the Father right now, gently putting His hand under your chin and lifting your head up, looking you in the eyes and saying, "You're forgiven."

His Word says that if we confess our sins He is faithful and just to forgive us and make our lives clean. (1 John 1:9.)

Psalm 51:7 NLT says:

> Purify me from my sins, and I will be clean; wash me, and I will be whiter than snow.

I grew up in western Canada and spent a lot of time in the mountains. There is nothing like a fresh snowfall, when everything is completely covered in at least a foot of snow. It's so beautiful and sparkling clean. It just glistens.

When we've sinned (and we all know when we have), it's absolutely our responsibility as God's daughter to ask the Lord to forgive us, to receive His forgiveness, and in some cases to ask others to forgive us. When we do, we are just like that snow—clean and glowing.

> Come now, and let us reason together, saith the Lord: though your sins be as scarlet, they shall be as white as snow;

though they be red like crimson, they shall be as wool.

Isaiah 1:18

One time when I was about 16 and had just started driving, some of us were hanging out and talking in front of a friend's house. A boy from school pulled up, and we were all talking to him at his car. As he was leaving, he backed up to turn around and backed right into my car. Then he told me not to tell my dad and mom because he didn't have insurance. Because he was a senior football player and I was a little intimidated by him, I agreed to tell my parents that it must have happened in the school parking lot and that I didn't have a clue who did it.

I went home and proceeded to lie to my parents, but I felt sick. I couldn't sleep that night, and I was sick to my stomach the next day at school. I loved my parents, and I had been a Christian for a couple of years so I knew I had sinned. God's daughters don't lie.

I couldn't wait to get home from school that day to tell the truth. On my way, I pulled over in my

'66 red Chevy and prayed, "Lord, please forgive me for lying, and give me the courage and strength to tell my parents the truth...and don't let that boy beat me up." (He was a big boy—and not a very nice one.)

When I prayed, I knew I was on the right track but still had to obey God's Word and honor my parents by telling them the truth. I knew there would be consequences, but I also knew I was going to be able to hold my head up again. Doing the right thing and facing the punishment I would receive was so much better than walking around ashamed!

If I'd kept the lie going, what kind of a witness would that have been to the boy and all the other people who knew I was a Christian—including my own family, whom I was trying to reach?

Had I ever blown it just because I was afraid of a middle linebacker! I found out that day that no matter how much you think you've blown it with God, He is always faithful to His Word. The minute I told my parents the truth, the words "white as snow," "clean," "forgiven," and "right-standing" all became more real to me than ever—and I was relieved! I felt like a new girl.

I still hadn't faced that boy, but because I had done what was right, I wasn't afraid anymore. My parents forgave me, and the boy had to pay to fix my car. Thankfully, he didn't beat me up, but I did get a few dirty looks from him the rest of the school year!

Whenever you've been shown mercy, it can't stop there. The Lord wants you to hold your head up so you can help others hold their heads up, look into their eyes, and show them God's love, His truth, and His mercy. That's what it's all about.

God gave His Son, Jesus, who shed His blood so you and I can stand forgiven and unashamed with our head held high, so we can help heal a hurting world. I know you want to be that kind of young woman.

think pink

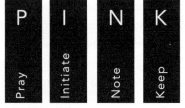

P — Pray
I — Initiate
N — Note
K — Keep

Lord, I just want to thank You for forgiving me of all my sins and washing me white as snow. I don't have to be ashamed, because You forgive me and are so patient with me. I love You!

Keep your thoughts
right—for as you think,
so you are. Thoughts are
things; therefore, think
only the things that will
make the world better and
you unashamed.

—Henry H. Buckley[vi]

3 things you must tell your parents

Communication is the key to victory in any kind of relationship. Great companies, great armies, great churches, great sports teams, and great homes all have one thing in common: They have learned to communicate effectively with one another. Communication is not talking. It is listening, observing, studying, and, finally, talking. People who only learn to talk are not communicating; they are spewing. To open up good communication lines with your parents, there are 3 things you must always tell them.

⭐ *Tell them when you need help.*

It may be in school, a relationship, or a job, but if you need help and guidance, let your parents know. That's why God gave them to you—to help you get through tough times.

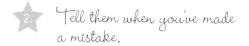

2 ✦ *Tell them when you've made a mistake.*

It might be easier at the time to try to cover it up, but honesty not only will help you avoid this same mistake in the future; it will also earn you big points in the "trust quest."

3 ✦ *Tell them you love and appreciate them.*

Sure, there's no such thing as a perfect parent, but most have made a very significant investment of time, energy, and money in their children. Regularly let your parents know you love them, even if they don't always show the same love in return.

gen·er·ous

liberal in giving

characterized by a noble or forbearing spirit[xvii]

You're never too young to be generous. It always means so much to me when my sons are generous with a cheerful heart. I just want to do a little jig. That's the kind of giving your parents notice. It makes us so grateful—so very grateful!

You're not too young to give at home. Give to your brothers and sisters. I'm not talking about money or gifts. I'm talking about just acknowledging them, being thoughtful to listen to them. You may have different interests, so just take a little time to listen to their hopes and dreams. Pray for them. Be kind to their friends. All these things go a long way.

Another place where you're not too young to give is in church. Find out where you can serve. Maybe you can help in the nursery. Maybe you can sing.

You might be one of those greeting types. Giving of your time is so generous.

I also want to talk to you about tithing. I learned about tithing when I was about 14 years old. I need to tell you, once you start to tithe, if you haven't already, you're in for the gift that keeps on giving.

Malachi 3:10 NIV says, "'Bring the whole tithe into the storehouse, that there may be food in my house. Test me in this,' says the Lord Almighty, 'and see if I will not open the floodgates of heaven and pour out so much blessing that you will not have room enough for it.'"

The tithe is 10 percent of your income, and it's important to understand that part of being God's daughter is being obedient to His Word. You might think it sounds a little crazy, but God even says to *test*, or *prove*, Him in this.

All I can say is *just do it*, and watch how He will give you wisdom with the rest of your money. He'll even give you ideas on how to make money. It's wonderful to know that you are trusting God with something you've worked hard for, that you've given something you put your heart into. Now, that's giving. Commit to do this. You'll be blessed, and you'll be a part of blessing your church.

Being a generous friend is something God expects you to be, too. Be the kind of friend that you want your friends to be to you. Sometimes a good way to decide how to help your friends is to put yourself in their shoes. What would it be like to be in their circumstances? Just ask the Lord to give you ideas and wisdom.

God wants you to give more than you even want to, because when you're generous with your time, your money, your gifts, and your talents, people see the love of God that's been shed abroad in your heart by the Holy Spirit—and that's exactly what it's there for: to give!

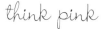

think pink

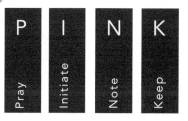

P — Pray
I — Initiate
N — Note
K — Keep

Just out of the blue, ask your mom, dad, brother, or sister if there is anything you can do for them. Even better, just do something for them that you know will help them out. Surprise them. What a way to show God's love!

All the flowers of tomorrow are in the seeds that we sow today!

—Unknown Author

3 ways helping your parents helps you

"What do I get out of this?"

I'm glad you asked. Perhaps you get an allowance that you can point to as some form of payment for your help with the family chores. But maybe not. We've never had a regular allowance with any of our teenagers, but they've always worked very willingly because they care about our family and understand that rewards will come. So here are 3 ways helping out Mom and Dad will help you even more.

1. Welcome to training camp for life's big leagues.

I'm so glad now that my parents instilled great work habits in me when I was a teenager. They gave me all that I would need to make my bosses happy and get me many raises along the way.

2 *You are sowing seed that you will harvest in your own home one day.*

I believe one of the reasons my 3 boys have always been good workers in our home is that I was a good worker in my house. The Bible says that God is never mocked and that any time a seed of any kind is sown, you will reap in due season. (Gal. 6:7.)

3 *Helping Mom and Dad gives you favor with them.*

It won't be long until you really need something from your parents. Every willing, well-done work puts another good deposit in your favor account with them. Withdrawals are easier when you've put something in the bank.

hon-or

one's word given as a guarantee of performance; integrity

one whose worth brings respect or fame

Ephesians 6:1 NIV says, "Children (daughters), obey your parents in the Lord, for this is right. Honor your father and mother"—which is the first commandment with a promise—"that it may go well with you and that you may enjoy long life on the earth."

I'm sure some of you can quote this Scripture backwards, forwards, and inside out. But if not, it's never too late to put this one in your heart. It really goes without saying how important it is for us, as God's daughters and daughters to our parents, to obey this. It is one of the Ten Commandments, so that says something.

The Lord wouldn't ask us to do this if it weren't going to benefit us, just as the Scripture says. God promises us that if we obey and honor our parents, it will go well with us and we'll enjoy a long life on the earth. He also wouldn't ask us to do this if it weren't possible.

Notice that the Scripture says, "Obey your parents *in the Lord.*" You are not required to obey any parent or authority figure who tells you to do something that goes against the Word of God. Most parents are trying their best. Both my husband and I grew up with parents who didn't know the Lord. If you're in the same situation, then you have a perfect opportunity to show the love of God. Honoring them is the best way.

If you don't have Christian parents, please know that even the strongest of Christian families have struggles. As a mom of three great and good boys, I've messed up so many times. I thank God for His mercy and for the forgiveness and under-standing of my kids. Please tell me you'll forgive your parents, and don't ever give up on them! Speak well of them, pray for them, and show them respect.

Offer the same honor to the other authority figures in your life as well, such as grandparents, pastors, teachers, and coaches. Tell these people you appreciate them.

Tell your dad and mom you love them. I don't think you can ever tell your family you love them too much. Your family might not be really affectionate, but you can get the ball rolling. Pass out some hugs once in a while.

Show your dad and mom you love them by helping out. Whatever God has asked you to do, He has without a doubt given you the ability to do it. He wouldn't ask us to obey our parents if He didn't think we were capable. Ask the Lord to help you. Ask Him to show you His heart towards your dad and mom. Shock them. Go for it. Clean that room. Empty that dishwasher. Go the extra mile! It's the little things that will bless their socks off, and you'll feel pretty good about yourself too. And the Lord will say, "That's My daughter!"

We need to do our best to be Christ-like at home. Your dad, mom, brothers, sisters—and pets, too—need to know that God loves them. The Bible says that as Jesus is, so are we to this world. His love and kindness flow through us.

It's been said that who you are at home is the real you! That's a thought. Let the Lord help you be His ambassador in your home by honoring your parents. You can do all things through Christ who gives you strength!

think pink

P — Pray
I — Initiate
N — Note
K — Keep

COLOSSIANS

3:20 AMP

*Children, obey your parents
in everything, for this is
pleasing to the Lord.*

Be not ashamed of thy virtues; honor's a good brooch to wear in a man's hat at all times.

—Ben Jonson[ix]

7 things a parent loves in a teenager

The Bible tells us that a wise child will make her father happy, but a foolish child will cause her mother grief. (Prov. 10:1.) The attitudes and actions you display in your home can have a major influence on the happiness of your family.

Here are 7 things you can do to bring joy in your family.

 1. Do your chores without someone asking you to do them.

 2. Offer to help with something around the house that is not usually your responsibility.

 3. Think of a compliment you can give your mom or dad, or both.

Ask your parents if there is anything you can do to improve your behavior.

 When asked to do something, don't procrastinate even a minute. Go right to it.

 If you have a brother or sister, treat your sibling with the same respect that you would want in return.

 Be polite, thoughtful, and helpful outside of your home: at school, at church, and in other activities.

thank-ful

expressive of thanks

well pleased: glad

The Bible says, "Every time I think of you, I give thanks to my God" (Phil. 1:3 NLT). Even though I might not know you, I truly am thankful for you. As I prepared to write these devotions, I prayed for all the young women who would read this book. In prayer, I have thanked God for you, that you are growing closer to your heavenly Father every day, and that this book will help you.

I, myself, don't have any daughters. I have 3 wonderful sons. Some of my dearest friends have daughters, whom I just love, and I also have 3 precious nieces who are very sweet and a lot of fun to be around.

I am thankful for all of the women whom God has blessed my life with. I am so thankful for moms, daughters, sisters, grandmas, aunts, cousins, nieces, and girlfriends. Without all of us, God wouldn't have His daughters, and we wouldn't have each other. The world just wouldn't be the same without us. God bless His girls!

As we talk about thankfulness, let me ask you a question.

Would you rather hang around people who are thankful or unthankful?

Take a moment to think about the times you have been around ungrateful, complaining people. It's not very much fun. What's really bad is if you're one of them!

Have you ever stopped and listened to yourself? You can't possibly get away from you. But you can take a good look at your heart and mind, and you can ask the Lord to help you change your attitude.

I think we've all been guilty of being unthankful from time to time. I've caught myself several times, just by myself, grumbling to myself. It's so not beautiful. That's why the Word of God says to not worry about anything but instead make our requests known to God. He also says to give thanks in everything. That doesn't mean to thank God for everything bad. It means that even in unpleasant circumstances, we can still have a thankful heart because our trust is in a good Father!

Make up your mind to be a thankful person. Settle it once and for all. It just has to be done. Not only will you like being around yourself, but others will also want to be around you.

This is a good time to bring up manners. Appreciation is so much a part of being a godly young woman. Saying "thank you" to people means so much. You know, don't you, how nice it is to receive a thank-you note? It means a lot to just be gracious and say "thank you" to your server or the little gal at the mall who helped you. You might be that little gal who works at the mall or restaurant. Oh, how your feet ache and you just want to go home! It means a lot to you to hear someone say, "Thank you so much. Have a nice day."

Being God's daughters isn't about being self-centered or just about what God and everyone else can do for us. Instead, let's think about what God can do through us for others. I guarantee you that with that attitude, you won't be able to help but be a very thankful, grateful young woman.

Let's do it. Let's be the most thankful girls in town!

I wish I could meet you and give you a big hug and say, "Thank you for reaching out to others with a heart full of thanks!"

think pink

PHILIPPIANS

4 : 6 NIV

Do not be anxious about anything,
but in everything, by prayer and
petition, with thanksgiving, present
your requests to God.

A thankful heart is not
only the greatest virtue,
but also the parent of
all other virtues.

—Cicero[xi]

3 reasons your relationship with your parents will affect your career

Your relationship with your parents is simply preparation for the rest of your life experiences, including work and career. There are at least 3 important reasons why your career will either succeed or fail as a direct result of how you get along with the authority in your house.

If you can't honor and obey those who love you in your home, it's unlikely that you'll behave any better with a boss who won't be nearly as likely to forgive.

Remember: Your parents will be the last bosses you have who can't fire you.

Your parents have already been where you are headed.

They have experienced the real world. If you're smart, you'll ask questions, listen to their experiences and wisdom, and learn what it takes to succeed.

 There will be times when school, chores, and life at home will seem boring and redundant.

The day will come when you will experience the same feelings with your job and career. Learning to persevere and rejuvenate your passion will put you ahead of the pack.

en-cour-age

to inspire with courage, spirit, or hope

to spur on: stimulate[xii]

Being an encourager is a very important job God has given us. We can learn everything we need to know about encouraging others by looking at Him. The Bible says our Father is an encourager:

> All praise to the God and Father of our Master, Jesus the Messiah! Father of all mercy! God of all healing counsel! He comes alongside us when we go through hard times, and before you know it, he brings us alongside someone else who is going through hard times so that we can be there for that person just as God was there for us.
>
> *2 Corinthians 1:3,4 MSG*

I hope and pray that you've known what it's like to be encouraged. I pray that as you read these devotions you know more than ever how great you are and how precious you are to God. We all need to hear that!

Some people are just naturally very comfortable at encouraging others, while some have to work a little harder at it. Let me take just a moment to encourage you right now that you can do it! You can cheer people on.

The Bible says, "A word aptly spoken is like apples of gold in settings of silver" (Prov. 25:11 NIV). Another version of this Scripture says, "The right word at the right time is like a custom-made piece of jewelry" (MSG). Take your pick: gold apples or lovely jewelry. Both sound good to me!

Just remember: The Lord is counting on us to speak good, kind, uplifting, helpful, comforting words to people; words that bring hope and faith. Our words can change someone's life.

God's Word also says, "Words kill, words give life; they're either poison or fruit—you choose" (Prov. 18:21 MSG).

Besides speaking kind words, there are other ways to encourage people.

Words can be put on a little note. I have received notes that I've read over and over. It might have taken that person 2 minutes to write it, but it will help me for a lifetime.

A smile goes a long, long way.

A compliment does too!

A little gift lets a person know you're thinking of them and that you and God love them and care! (It doesn't have to be expensive. Maybe it could be a little candle or a tiny picture frame.)

Tell someone you'll pray for them. Now, remember: You mean business. If you say you're going to pray, then pray! A good idea, if possible, is to pray for them right then and there!

Make a phone call. As you're going through your day, a person may come to mind not just once but several times. Sometimes you need to stop and pray for them. Often you could just give them a quick phone call and say, "I've just been thinking about you. Is there anything I can do for you?"

A quick little e-mail can encourage someone too. The e-mails I send have to be quick because my typing isn't that great. "Short and sweet" is a good e-mail motto.

These are all ways that our Father can use us to encourage others.

Now, how can you get encouraged?

Well, I believe God will speak to others to encourage you, but the very best way is to try to remember to go to Him first. He's your Father. He knows you better than you know yourself and knows exactly what you need. He can encourage you like no one else. I love the saying "Go to the throne (God's throne) before you go to the phone."

As God's daughter, you are privileged to enter into His throne room. When you're discouraged, it takes faith to enter His gates with thanksgiving and His courts with praise. You might not feel like it, and that's why I say it takes faith. Get your Bible out, and read some psalms out loud. Faith comes from hearing the Word of God. Sometimes we just gotta do it!

When you're discouraged, that's the time to run to your heavenly Father. Don't run away. His love and His Word never fail. Hope and faith will begin to rise up in you. Trust in the Lord with all your heart; don't lean on your own understanding. In all your ways acknowledge Him, and He will direct your path. He'll show you steps to take.

We can learn to encourage ourselves in the Lord! Let me tell you, that's a true sign of growing up!

Don't you worry. If you've asked the Lord to help you, help is on its way. Don't limit Him! Nothing can stop His love from getting to you. (Rom. 8:38-40.) He wants His daughter encouraged and equipped and strong so you don't miss out on the wonderful plans He has for you. I'm so excited for you! God bless you, you daughter of the Most High God!

think pink

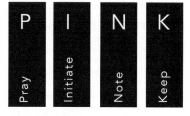

P — Pray
I — Initiate
N — Note
K — Keep

Think about someone you would like to encourage. Write them a note, and let them know what they mean to you. Remind them of how much God loves them and you love them. It only takes a minute, but it can make someone's day— even change their life.

Kind words can be
short and easy to speak,
but their echoes are
truly endless.

—Mother Theresa[xiii]

encourager

Let no corrupt word proceed out of your mouth, but what is good for necessary edification, that it may impart grace to the hearers.

Ephesians 4:29 NKJV

A little girl came home from a tough day at school and collapsed onto the sofa in her living room. She sighed to herself out loud: "Nobody loves me. The whole world hates me!" Her little brother, who was in the room playing video games, responded, "That's not true, Sis. Some people don't even know you."

He'd had a great opportunity to give some encouraging words to his sister, but instead he'd only added to her frustrations.

If you want people to seek you out as a friend, then be an encourager. It takes a great person to see past people's shortcomings to find the good things and praise them.

re-la-tion-ship

the state of being related or interrelated

kinship [xiii]

In the introduction of this little book we talked about many different hats we wear as God's daughters: daughters to our heavenly Father, daughters to our earthly parents, sisters, grand-daughters, nieces, cousins, friends, best friends, students, and the list goes on.

First things first: Our #1 relationship is with our heavenly Father.

One thing God gave us when He made us was a longing to be loved. Did you know there is not one single person in the whole world who can completely fill that longing in your heart? We all do depend on others to fill that longing and hunger in our hearts. But nobody on earth can do it for you: not your family, not your friends, not that prince charming you dream of one day marrying—nope, not even him. And guess what. You will do your best to love your husband and the children God blesses you with, but we all fall short. That's why your first love should be to the Lord. His love never fails, and His love also helps cover our failures.

God first loved us. He chose us to receive His salvation. When we receive that love, we become His daughters. I'll never forget the first time I knew that God loved me.

I was sitting in my room thinking about how many times I had disappointed my dad and mom. I was about 13 or 14 (I wish I had written down the date), and I was with my friends, drinking, smoking, and probably cussing. (It wasn't the first time.) My parents didn't know what I'd been up to, and for some reason (maybe someone was praying) I felt worse than I'd ever felt about myself. I wanted to change so bad but didn't know how. I had been to Sunday school when I was little and sometimes went to church Christmas Eve and Easter Sunday, and I had seen Billy Graham on TV. I was very conscious of God and believed in Him.

I knew there was a Bible on the bookshelf in our family room that my Uncle Freddie and Auntie Ruby had given my dad and mom a couple years prior. I got that precious Bible, sat on my bed, and read Scriptures about God's love until about 4 A.M. There was a section in the front of this Bible that told how to become a born-again Christian. I read and read—and read some more. I cried, and cried some more—first tears of sorrow and then, for an even longer time, tears of joy (real, true joy). I felt so clean and so pure—so forgiven.

From that day forward until this day, no one—not anyone—can ever take away that knowledge of God's love. I knew that I knew that I knew He loved me, and for the first time I had an understanding of what Jesus had done for me. (Rom. 8:15,16.) That night changed my life forever.

Receiving God's love comes by reading and hearing God's Word (His love letters to His daughters) and by prayer (talking to Him and listening to Him). Reading the Word, hearing the Word at church, and praying are things you can do to grow in faith and in the knowledge of God's absolute love for you.

When we make Jesus the Lord of our lives, we are adopted into God's family. He really is our Father. When we are born again, God's Spirit (the Holy Spirit) touches our spirit and tells us who we are and whom we belong to. You are God's daughter. As you gain understanding of that acceptance and love, you will bless others.

Remember: As a daughter, sister, friend, granddaughter, cousin, niece, auntie, wife, mother, grandmother—all you've been called to be in all of your relationships—you will flourish because you, my dear friend, have made the choice to receive the love of God through His Son Jesus. Therefore, you have something so amazing to give: You'll give His best. As God's daughter, you are blessed to be a blessing!

think pink

P I N K

Pray Initiate Note Keep

JOHN 1:12 NIV

Yet to all who received him, to
those who believed in his name,
he gave the right to become
children of God.

Cherish your human
connections: your
relationships with
friends and family.

—Barbara Bush[xv]

4 ways to tell parents "thank you"

As you grow in your relationships, I believe one of the greatest character traits that you can develop in your life is appreciation and gratefulness towards others. It's important that you find practical ways to show gratitude to someone who has been a blessing to you. Nothing warms my heart more as a mom than when one of my boys takes the time to tell me and their dad "thanks" for something we've done for them. Here are some ways you can say "thanks."

1. A card.

Take the time to write out your feelings towards your parents, accounting for the specific things they've done that you are grateful for.

2. A gift.

It doesn't have to be expensive. Maybe it's a gift certificate to their favorite restaurant or store. A small sacrifice of finances on your part communicates a big message to Mom and Dad.

3. *Unexpected work.*

Do something around the house you weren't asked to do: the trash, the dishes, the yard—whatever. Tell them you just wanted to find a way to say thanks.

4. *Go ahead and tell them.*

Say it out loud, and say it whenever they've done something good for you: a good meal, permission to use the car, a night at the movies—whatever it might be. Tell them, "Thanks!"

a letter from Dad

Before I shaped you in the womb, I knew all about you. I know when you leave and when you get back. You're never out of My sight. I know you inside and out. I know every bone in your body. I know exactly how you were made, bit by bit; how you were sculpted from nothing into something. Like an open book, you grew from conception to birth before Me. All the stages of your life were spread out before Me. The days of your life were all prepared before you'd even lived one day. (Jer. 1:5; Ps. 139:3,15,16.)

I created you in My own image, to reflect My nature. I paid greater attention to you than to any of My creation, down to the last detail—even numbering the hairs on your head! You are My masterpiece. I have created you anew in Christ Jesus, so that you can do the good things I planned for you long ago. I have lavished a Father's love upon you, just because you are My child! I want you to clearly know the plans I have for you. My plan is to prosper you; never to harm you, but to give you hope and a future. (Gen. 1:27; Matt. 10:30; Eph. 2:10; 1 John 3:1; Jer. 29:11.)

Every gift I give you will be good and perfect. I will never change My mind about My desire to help you. If you will simply delight yourself in Me, I will give you the desires and secret petitions of your heart. Call to Me, and I will always answer you. In fact, I'll tell you marvelous and wondrous things that you could never figure out on your own. Remember: I can do anything—far more than you could ever imagine or guess or request in your wildest dreams! I do it by working within you. (James 1:17; Ps. 37:4; Jer. 33:3; Eph. 3:20.)

If your heart is broken, I'll be right there. I'll save you when you are crushed in your spirit. I will care for you like a Shepherd. You are a lamb in My arms, held close to My heart. I'll wipe every tear from your eyes. If you ever doubt My love, remember that I loved you so much that I gave the only Son I had, Jesus, to lay down His life, just so you could live with Me forever. I hope you are absolutely convinced that absolutely nothing—nothing living or dead, angelic or demonic, today or tomorrow, high or low, thinkable or unthinkable—can get between you and My love, because of what Jesus did for you. And one day I look forward to seeing you face to face: tears gone, crying gone, pain gone. Remember that I am coming soon, so keep living by all the words you find in My book. (Ps. 34:18; Isa. 40:11; Rev. 21:4; John 3:16; Rom. 8:38,39; Rev. 21:4,7.)

Love,
Dad...Your Father in Heaven

a daughter's prayer

Father, I come to You, in the name of Jesus, and I thank You for loving me and choosing me to be Your daughter. You gave Your Son Jesus for me. He gave His life so that I can live eternally with You and for You. I know I don't deserve all that You have done for me, so that makes me even more grateful to receive Your love and to know that I belong to You.

I delight myself in You. I trust in You with all of my heart. I don't want to try to figure out everything on my own. I want to hear Your voice in every decision I have to make. I know You will direct me. Thank You for placing Your desires for me in my heart.

Thank You for showing me the right people to follow—people who will teach me and challenge me to be more like Jesus. Help me to be an example to others. I am honored to represent You to this world as I follow Jesus.

I am so thankful that I can come to You with all of my sins and You forgive me. When I lay my head on my pillow at night, I have such peace—a peace only You can give because You've made my heart clean. That makes me want to praise You so much. I know when my feet hit the floor in the morning it's like a new beginning, and because my eyes and heart look to You, I can hold my head high. You give me confidence to take on another day.

Help me to be a giver, Lord. Show me ways to give of myself—my money, my time, and my talents. I want to be Your most generous daughter. You have blessed me to be a blessing.

Let me start right here at home by honoring and obeying my parents. I don't always understand them, and I know they don't always get me, but I trust Your Word. Thank You for Your grace to obey. I know when I give honor and obedience to my parents, it brings honor to You. Thank You for my family, Lord. I don't ever want to take them for granted. Show me ways to be helpful. I choose to speak kind words to my family. One way to bring honor to You and my parents is to be good to my siblings. You have put Your love in my heart so I can be the sister and daughter You have called me to be.

Father, teach me to pray and to worship You in spirit and truth. Spending time with You and hiding Your Word in my heart is what I want to do so my cup runs over to others. They'll know I've been in Your presence. They'll know how thankful I am that You are my Father. I want to be known as a very gracious and thankful young woman. You are so good to me, and I want to tell everyone of Your faithfulness in my life. Use me to encourage people and help them the way You and others have helped me.

More than anything, I desire to grow in the knowledge of You, Father. I want to grow in Your love and Your wisdom. Your Word is a lamp to my feet and a light to my path. As I walk on Your path, help me to be a daughter who pleases You in my relationships with my family and friends and to be a daughter who, above all else, demonstrates Your love and power to those who have yet to call upon the name of Jesus.

Thank You for choosing me to tell others how much You love them and to help You heal their broken hearts. You said in Your Word that the one who wins souls is wise. I don't want anyone to not know the love You've given me. Help me to be a wise daughter leading others to You.

I *delight* in the Lord.

I *aspire* to be someone others aspire to be.

I am *unashamed.*

I am a *generous* daughter.

I *honor* my parents and obey them.

I am *thankful.*

I *encourage* and am an encourager.

My *relationships* abound in God's love.

every teen girl's
little pink book
on girlfriends

Dear friend,

You are a dear friend, and I am so honored that you would take the time to read what I have written. With every little story and every Scripture I share, I pray that you will be encouraged.

This little pink book is all about girlfriends. Good, old-fashioned, true-blue, loyal, caring, sharing, fun-loving, devoted, kindhearted, sent-from-heaven, dearly loved girlfriends! That's the kind I want to be. How about you?

I hope the girlfriends you have can be described in such a way. It takes one to know one! Every good and perfect gift is from above. What a gift our girlfriends are, and we can be that same gift to them!

Love,
Cathy

sisters

Sisters can be absolutely the best friends you have, and friends are definitely like sisters. Don't ever feel left out if you don't have a sister. You really have many sisters. As a Christian, you are a sister in Christ to your other Christian girlfriends. It's called the Sisterhood!

I am very thankful for my little sister. She is six years younger than me. When we were growing up, that seemed to be quite a gap. We didn't have as much in common. We've always loved each other, but now that we're older we have so much fun together. We love to laugh, and we have taught each other different things. She is a great cook. My family loves when Jo Jo comes. She lives in Canada, and I live in Texas, but that has never stopped us from talking on the phone several times a week and will never stop me from thinking of her and praying for her every day.

I also have two wonderful sister-in-laws whom I love and admire so much. They are both awesome wives and mothers, and I really enjoy every moment we spend together.

What a wonderful thing to be able to pick up the phone and share good news with your sisters and girlfriends! It is as precious to me today as it was when I was your age.

God bless all of the wonderful women in our lives!

I received this little story in an email from a good friend and thought it was a good way to start this book.

A young wife sat on a sofa on a hot, humid day, drinking iced tea and visiting with her mother. As they talked about life, about marriage, about the responsibilities of life and the obligations of adulthood, the mother clinked the ice cubes in her glass thoughtfully and turned a clear, sober glance upon her daughter.

"Don't forget your sisters," she

advised, swirling the tea leaves to the bottom of her glass. "They'll be more important as you get older. No matter how much you love your husband, no matter how much you love the children you may have, you are still going to need sisters. Remember to go places with them now and then; do things with them. And remember that 'sisters' also means your girlfriends, your daughters, and other women relatives too. You'll need other women. Women always do."

What a funny piece of advice! the young woman thought. *Haven't I just gotten married? Haven't I just joined the couple world? I'm now a married woman, for goodness' sake! A grownup. Surely my husband and the family we may start will be all I need to make my life worthwhile!*

But she listened to her mother. She kept contact with her sisters and made more women friends each year. As the years tumbled by, one after another, she gradually came to understand that her mom really knew what she was talking about.

As time and nature work their changes and their mysteries upon a woman, sisters are the mainstays of her life.

After more than 50 years of living in this world, here is what I've learned:

Time passes.
Life happens.
Distance separates.
Children grow up.
Jobs come and go.
Parents die.
Colleagues forget favors.
Careers end.
But...

Girlfriends are there, no matter how much time and how many miles are between you. A girlfriend is never farther away than needing her can reach. When you have to walk that lonesome valley and you have to walk it by yourself, your girlfriends will be on the valley's rim, cheering you on, praying for you, pulling for you, intervening on your behalf, and waiting with open arms at the valley's end. Sometimes they will even break the rules and walk beside you—or come in and carry you out.

Author Unknown

think pink

P — Pray

I — Initiate

N — Note

K — Keep

PROVERBS 27:9 NLT

The heartfelt counsel of
a friend is as sweet as
perfume and incense.

You can kid the world.
But not your sister.

—Charlotte Gray[i]

3 marks of a true friend

There is a big difference between an acquaintance and a true friend. People you simply hang out with will come and go, but a true friend is someone who will always be there for you. Recognizing the difference will help you develop relationships that will last. Here are 3 traits of a true friend.

 **1** *Honesty.*

A true friend will tell you the truth no matter what, even if it may initially hurt your feelings. Having someone who will give you an honest answer is priceless. (Prov. 27:6.)

2 *Dependability.*

The people who truly value their friendship with you will keep their word. If you cannot count on someone, or if they cannot count on you, your friendship will not last.

3. Respect.

Mutual respect is a large part of a good friendship. If someone is not respected, their opinions and feelings will be discounted and overlooked. Without respect, a friendship will simply not work.

will you be my friend?

It is better to have no friends than to have the wrong friends. Remember: When you choose your friends, you are actually choosing your future. Don't settle for anything less than God's best for you. Be patient. He will knit your heart together with those who will help you grow—girlfriends who are like-minded and who want to please the Lord, just as you do. They will help you grow, and you will do the same for them.

I have heard it said this way: *It's good to have friends you can learn from.* It's a wonderful thing to have great godly women whom you can follow. When they have been where you're headed, they challenge you to grow. We can learn so much from others if we humble ourselves and wait on them and listen to them.

We also need to keep ourselves in a place where our younger sisters and girlfriends can learn from us. Make yourself available to the Lord so He can use you to be a leader of other young women. Someone is always watching you.

I remember deciding at one time that I was not the leader type. I didn't want to be a *leader*. That word scared me. Then one day I heard someone say that we are all leaders. There is always someone following us. I found out that just by being a mother I was automatically a leader. I had three little ones watching me all day every day.

You have little sisters, little cousins, and little neighbor girls watching you. Several years after I had grown up, a former neighbor girl told me that my life had influenced her. She was ten years younger than me. I was honored, and more than anything I felt such a sense of responsibility! It made me realize how important it is to be an example, even while you're young. Set an example for others by what you say and do, as well as by your love, faith, and purity!

You are too valuable to sell yourself short by spending precious time with people who don't really care for you. God is faithful and has promised wonderful relationships for you. This little pink book is about girlfriends, but remember that every relationship in your life can be blessed if you only ask the Lord to help you and lead you to choose wonderful friends and to be a true friend to others.

think pink

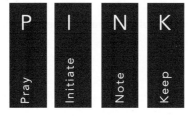

P I N K

Pray

Initiate

Note

Keep

Lord, help me to choose wise friends. I want friends who love You. I know I need friends who will help me grow closer to You. I want to be a friend who encourages them, too. Lord, show me how to pray for my friends and to be sensitive to help them. I really want to be supportive in my actions and in my words. Thank You for my friends.

In the cookies of life,
friends are the
chocolate chips.

—Author Unknown

girlfriend

⭐ **Gift** — Your friends are a gift from God, so treat them that way.

⭐ **Inspire** — Inspire each other to do big things.

⭐ **Rally** — Rally around each other. You need to comfort your friends when they are hurting, and be happy for them when they have something to celebrate.

⭐ **Listen** — When your friend talks, listen to what she's saying. This is the easiest and most important part of being a good friend.

⭐ **Fun** — This is the best part of having friends!

⭐ **Real** — Keep it real. Don't be fake. True friends will see right through it.

⭐ **Include** — Expand your group of friends, and get to know others because they can influence your life, too.

Eternal — Make sure you and your friends spend eternity together by sharing the gift of Jesus with them.

Nice — Show kindness and forgiveness to your friends, even if you don't feel like they deserve it sometimes.

Dream — Dream together. Dream about your future and what you want to accomplish in life.

growing
good
friends

Make it a goal that your girlfriends will be better off after spending time with you, just as you are better off after spending time with the Lord.

Plant good seed in your friendship soil. Help your friends grow. Girls are natural nurturers. God made us to want to help others grow. We love to care for and look after others. Many of us liked caring for our baby dolls. As little girls, we were little mothers from the get-go! That is a good thing—as long as we don't get too bossy with our girlfriends! We need to just help each other and encourage one another as we listen to each other's dreams.

Have short Bible studies with your girlfriends. Pray for each other. Write out Scriptures to encourage them in areas they are struggling with. Be a friend who says:

"You can do it!"

"I'll help you."

"God is faithful."

"You are a blessing."

"Never, never, never give up."

"Let's pray."

Your girlfriends will be forever grateful for you!

I am so thankful for my girlfriends. Oh my goodness! I always hope I tell them enough how each of them has blessed my life! I thank God for every remembrance of these gals in my life! Thank You, Lord!

think pink

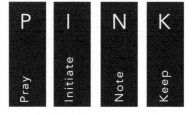

P — Pray
I — Initiate
N — Note
K — Keep

If you are having a hard time sharing God's love with someone, ask the Lord to help you see that person through His eyes. Ask Him to give you His heart for her. I guarantee you that when you pray like that, you'll know God's love is working in you and through you. He'll show you the next step. Remember: Hurting people hurt people. Try being kind to the mean girls, and see what happens!

"My best friend is the
one who brings out
the best in me."

—Henry Ford[ii]

3 messages that lift people up

We grow up in a down world. Comedian Jerry Seinfeld pokes fun at parents who are always using the word "down" with their children: "Get down!" "Settle down." Quiet down." "Turn that thing down!" You get the point. Many of the messages people hear in our world are not very positive. The nightly news is full of stories of war, crime, and tragedy.

When you have a message that encourages, you are sure to stand out from the crowd. Here are 3 messages you can share that will lift a person up.

1. *"God created you to succeed in life."*

But like any created thing, you must find out exactly what you were created to do. A hammer isn't very good at being a screwdriver, but it's powerful when used for its creative purpose.

2. *"No matter what you've done, Jesus Christ loves you without conditions."*

The Bible says that while we were yet sinners, Christ died for us. (Rom. 5:8.) When we were at our worst, Jesus gave us His very best.

3. *"Heaven is a little like earth, without the bad days."*

The Bible talks about streets, trees, and rivers in heaven. So there are similarities to earth. Yet it promises no pain and no tears! It is absent of tragedy, depression, and temptation. And God has a mansion prepared for every one of His children. (John 14:2; Rev. 21:4,21; Rev. 22:1,2.)

friends
forever

There is something so precious about the friends God knits our hearts together with. You watch! You are at an age when some girlfriends may come and go, but you are beginning friendships that are everlasting. They are eternal!

One of my fondest memories is when I was in the seventh grade—or as we said in Canada, grade 7. I had just moved to a new area in our city. I'd had good friends but had never really known what it was to have a best friend.

One day during summer vacation, my friend Laura and I were walking around a park in our neighborhood. We had gotten to know each other that year at school and always had so much fun together. I'm sure that morning I probably scared her a little, but I suddenly had this over-whelming urge to tell her that I considered her my best friend. So I did! She told me I was hers, too, and we were so happy that we hugged and cried a little. I think I skipped all the way home. I was so proud to have a "best friend" and to get to be one.

What is so amazing is that a couple years later we got saved. That made our friendship even more wonderful! When we grew up, we were in each other's weddings. We even both married ministers! Over the years we've lived so far apart, but our friendship is eternal. Sometimes a year or six months goes by before we talk on the phone, but every time we do we laugh and talk like we've never been apart. We can pray for each other, encourage one another, and laugh together, just as if we were back in the seventh grade again. All those miles and all those years will never change what the Lord did in our hearts that day. I love that!

You may have friendships even now that you already know will be forever. Treasure those friendships. We only have a few like that.

Sometimes you have to move away or your friends move away, but remember: Nothing can stop you from communicating these days. You can write letters, e-mail, or talk on the phone. You don't have to lose touch.

It is our responsibility to keep in touch with friends God has given us. We can't get too busy to show our friends we care. When those girlfriends come to mind, pray for them. There is no distance in prayer. There isn't!

Don't be one of those friends who says, "Well, she never calls me." Just be the one to initiate it. You'll be glad you did.

Think about this. Our girlfriends are our sisters in Christ, and we will continue our friendships in heaven forever and ever. That's what I'm talking about: eternal! We can all giggle together in heaven! God's daughters get to hang out together forever. Just think: no curfew! And we won't be cranky the next day after one of those crazy slumber parties! We get to enjoy our friendships now and forever!

think pink

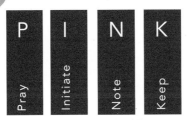

A good way to make sure you are being the best friend you can be is to compare yourself to Galatians 5:22-23. You should strive to have all of these qualities in your relationships with your friends:

Love   Goodness
Joy   Faithfulness
Peace   Gentleness
Patience   Self-control
Kindness

A good tree bears good fruit. None of us have perfected all of these fruits, but our Lord Jesus has, and He will help us in these areas when we ask Him to.

To the world you are just one person, but to one person, you could mean the world.

—Author Unknown[iii]

4 reasons it's critical that you listen to people

Many times, the best preaching and teaching that Christ did was a direct result of His listening to someone. People would come to Him with sometimes simple, and other times very difficult, questions. The Holy Spirit would give Jesus the answer every time. The Bible tells us to "be quick to listen, slow to speak" (James 1:19 NIV). A listening heart attracts many friends and will always be rewarded with wisdom from heaven. Here are 4 reasons to have a listening heart.

1 *Listening gives you time to fully evaluate a person's situation before you pass on counsel or advice that is premature.*

2 *Listening tells the person you care.* It says that person is important and you are not in a rush to send them away.

3. *Listening gives you time to hear from God.*

The Lord will speak to you clearly when you take unselfish interest in the lives of others.

4. *God believes in listening.*

What do you think He's doing when we pray? He's listening. Have you ever noticed that He gave us 2 ears and 1 mouth? We ought to listen twice as much as we talk.

unexpected friendships

When I was in high school, there was a lady in my neighborhood whose son had gotten saved. He began to act so different afterwards that she wanted to know what had happened to him. One night she followed him to church and she asked Jesus into her heart. Shortly after, her husband and her two other children did the same thing.

The boy was a good friend of mine, and as his mom started to study the Bible more and more, she had a desire to teach a Bible study to some of the neighborhood girls. I got to be one of those girls and this woman became one of my best friends. I always respected her as an older woman and as a mom, but because she took time to teach me the Word of God, pray with me, and help me in many of my own family crises, I began to admire her as a woman of God and a true friend.

Her and her husband genuinely loved young people and would always welcome us in their home, and I loved being there. I'll never forget when I was about 17 years old she taught us girls about the fruit of the Spirit (love, joy, peace, self-control, kindness, patience, goodness, faithfulness, and gentleness). I loved those Bible studies because I was so hungry to learn God's Word.

Through the next couple of years some of us went away to school, but we always kept in touch with her. She was so interested in our lives and I knew she would pray if I asked her to. Like I said, even though she was older, I considered her a friend because she blessed my life so much.

All these years her oldest son and I had been friends. One year that friendship turned to *really* good friends and, before I knew it, I went from calling her Mrs. Bartel to Mom!

We went from being friends to mother-in-law and daughter-in-law. Today, she introduces me to people as her daughter-in-love. We've never lost that friendship and she truly is one of my best "girlfriends," as well as a great mom and role model. That's a good combination!

I'm thankful she taught me about the fruit of the Spirit and how to pray (not knowing that one day I would be married to her son) which prepared me for quite a ride (it's okay if I say that, Blaine won't be reading this little pink book on girlfriends).

I sure love you, Mom (Miss Elaine). Thank you for being a wonderful mom to all your kids and a girlfriend to us daughters.

my savior, my friend

Our first and very best friend should be the Lord. God didn't have to, but He chose us. When we are born again, we are adopted and God calls us His sons and daughters. He also chooses to call us His friends.

I was thinking about my three boys. Blaine and I will always have a parent-child relationship with them. We will always be Mom and Dad to them, but as they've gotten older we are so proud to call them our best friends—and we pray that our friendship will continue to grow. What a privilege to be God's daughter and what an honor to have a friendship with Him.

Not only are you a daughter of God, but He has called you His friend. Jesus said, "I have called you friends, for everything that I learned from my Father I have made known to you" (John 15:15). Because of your friendship, you can share every secret with Jesus, and He will share secrets with you. As you reveal your true self to Jesus, He will reveal the mysteries of God to you. The Bible says that as you draw near to Him, He will draw near to you. (James 4:8.)

As you pray, read the Bible, and listen to people sharing His Word, you will come to know the Friend who will always be by your side, even in the middle of the night, even in your silliest or loneliest moments. Jesus is closer than a sister or a brother (Prov. 18:24), and He will always be our very best friend.

think pink

P — Pray
I — Initiate
N — Note
K — Keep

J O H N 1 5 : 1 3 N I V

*Greater love has no one
than this, that he lay down
his life for his friends.*

Good friends are like stars. You don't have to always see them, but you know they're always there.

—Author Unknown[iv]

true friend

A friend loves at all times, and a brother is born for adversity.

Proverbs 17:17 NIV

For six years after he graduated from New York's Fashion Institute of Technology, Calvin Klein could get nothing better than bad-paying jobs in New York's garment district. Resorting to working in his dad's grocery story for extra cash, he was far from the dream he'd envisioned for his life.

But a friend believed in young Calvin and gave him $10,000 in startup money to launch his own business. Today you can find Mr. Klein's name on clothing around the world. A true friend will love and help you, even when you are at your lowest point.

girls just want to have fun!

There is nothing like a night out with girlfriends, or maybe just that one special friend. We just have to set aside time for that. No one understands a good heart-to-heart talk or a good laugh like your girlfriends.

I'm not knocking the guys. I have three sons and one husband I love being with. One of the reasons I fell in love with my husband was that I thought he was so funny. We always had fun being together. He still makes me laugh every day. My sons are a lot like their dad. They all have a great sense of humor. I always enjoy getting to hang out with all of them.

As much fun as they are, though, I always make it a point to plan time with my girlfriends. I say *plan* because we really do have to make things happen. I know you know what I'm talking about! If you just say, "Let's get together," and don't come up with a plan, then it won't happen. If those friendships are valuable to us, then we have to make it a priority to keep in touch.

Just a few months back, a dear friend and I were talking about just that. She told me that she and her mom, sisters, aunts, and nieces decided to meet once a month for dinner. It was important to them that, no matter how busy they all were, they spent that time together. Every month a different girl would choose the meeting place. They enjoyed a great time together and caught up on each other's lives.

Right after my friend told me that, the girls in my family started to do the same thing. What a blessing! We've had so much fun. My nieces, Ashley, Brittany, and Savannah, have all had a turn planning the evening. One night we went to look at Christmas lights. Of course, we brought some snacks (definitely some chocolate), and we had so much fun. It's my turn next month, so I'm thinking about ice skating.

It doesn't have to cost anything. Just get together at someone's house to have a little visit. Maybe play some games or watch a movie. It doesn't need to be extravagant. The whole idea is to stay in touch.

The Lord really does knit your heart together with your family's and friends'. He made you to need each other. These are the girls who are going to pray for you when you need them. They are some of your best cheerleaders, your biggest fans. They counsel you and believe in your dreams with you. And all along the way, you're doing the same for them. Enjoy the relationships God has given you.

We need to be so thankful for the women in our lives: moms, sisters, aunties, grandmas, cousins, neighbor girls, friends at school, teachers, coaches, our youth pastors' wives, our pastors' wives, and, as we get older, our mothers-in-law, sisters-in-law, daughters, and daughters-in-law (I want three of those) and even granddaughters (I'll take some of those too!). Our lives wouldn't be the same without them. We need them, and they need us.

I know you can think of lots of ways to spend time together. When you live far apart, don't let that stop you from keeping in touch. We have no excuses these days. We can make a little phone call, send an e-mail, or write a good, old-fashioned letter. Mail is nice, especially when you put some photos in there. I love letters, because when you miss someone you can read them over and over. Remember: Praying for your friends, near or far, always helps to keep them close to your heart.

think pink

P I N K

Pray · Initiate · Note · Keep

PHILIPPIANS
1 : 3   NIV

I thank my God every time
I remember you.

A friend loves you
enough to share her
chocolate with you
when you're down!

The first Sunday in August is
National Friendship Day.

*Here are a few ideas to help
you celebrate!*

Send your friends a card, or call them and tell
them how much you appreciate their friendship.

Invite your friends over for a sleepover, and
eat lots of junk food!

Put together a photo album containing
pictures of you and your friends doing fun
things.

Make your friend a friendship bracelet, or
buy her a necklace with both your initials to
symbolize your friendship.

Get all dolled up and go out with your
friends for dinner and a movie or the theatre.

Go on a picnic and then bike riding, hiking, ice skating, or swimming together.

 Make a CD of your mutually favorite songs.

 Call a radio station and dedicate a song to your friends.

 Write a poem about all the things you like about your friend.

Give your friends a HUG!

a gift from God

Friendship is a gift— an amazing gift—we never want to take for granted. As a young woman, are you finding out that life really is all about our relationships? People are everywhere. They're in your family, at school, at church, at work, at the mall, at restaurants, and in your neighborhood.

When our heavenly Father made us, He intended for us to relate to others. First, we are to love God with all our heart, soul, mind, and strength. Second, we are to love our family, friends, and neighbors as we love ourselves. When we spend time with the Lord (in His Word, worshipping Him, praying, and being taught in a good church), we understand more and more how much He loves us. Having that relationship with God the Father through our Lord Jesus Christ is going to absolutely benefit every other relationship in our lives. When we realize how much God loves us, we can love ourselves and be the kind of friend He wants us to be.

I need to explain something. We are called to love everyone. We can't do that without the love of God in our hearts. I don't want to look down on others. I don't want to be a self-righteous hypocrite. Do you? I didn't think so! Be the girl who rescues others. Be a lifeline, help the mean girls, and don't ever give up on anyone.

The first step is to pray for people. When we find ourselves being critical of people, we need to stop and think, *I wonder if that person has ever had anyone pray for them.* Let's do it. Our heart will be changed, and so will theirs.

think pink

P I N K

Pray Initiate Note Keep

P R O V E R B S
1 8 : 2 4   N K J V

A [girl] who has friends must
[her]self be friendly.

"A friend is one who
walks in when others
walk out."

—Walter Winch[v]

3 secrets to making new friends

Everyone wants to be liked. People want friends, and even those who seem a little "stuck up" want to be friendly. So here are 3 secrets that will help you make new friends.

1. Be friendly.

It seems obvious, but many people get so focused on other things that they miss the people and possible relationships passing them by. Grab each opportunity to build new relationships by doing the small things that make it happen. Say "hello," introduce yourself, or simply smile. Make the first effort by showing yourself friendly. (Prov. 18:24.)

2. Focus on others.

People want to talk about things that matter to them. If you spend 4 hours talking about your bad day to someone you just met, don't be surprised if they start avoiding you. Make the effort to find out what they like and focus on things that you have in common.

3. Do kind things without looking for credit.

The simple principle of sowing and reaping works in friendships too. If you begin to go out of your way to sow into the lives of people, you will begin to reap the kind of friends that you want. (Gal. 6:7.)

are you a mean girl?

There is absolutely nothing wrong with having a great group of girlfriends! Naturally, you have some friends who are closer to you than others. The question is this: Are you a *mean girl* or a *kind girl*?

Mean girls are just plain mean. They're selfish, gossipy, back-biting, rude, backstabbing, cruel, hateful, and unkind—and that's just within their own little group. They are even more mean to those outside their clique.

Kind girls, on the other hand, are nice. They are helpful, loving, caring, considerate, compassionate, big-hearted, hospitable, generous, understanding, and tenderhearted. The thing that I think is very admirable about kind girls is that they don't hesitate to reach out beyond their circle. We need to always be thinking of ways to reach out to the new girl, the lonely girl, the sad girl, the girl who's made some big mistakes and needs help getting a fresh start. We can reach out to that mean girl, too, who just got kicked out of that group.

These are all potential girlfriends and sisters in Christ! Be a part of that group of girls—or be the girl—at your church, youth group, or school that has hope to offer. There are girls who walk into your church thinking, *This is my last hope to find real love and friendship.* You might be the one to offer that hope.

The Lord wants us to step out of our comfort zone and open our hearts and our circle of friends to others. Our heavenly Father is all about growing, adding, and multiplying. He loved the world (everyone) so much that He gave His one and only Son, that whoever believes in Him will not perish but have eternal life. God's will is that everyone be saved. As His daughters, we want that, too. So let's always be thoughtful of how to show others how good He is. When they find out, they won't want to live another day without Him.

think pink

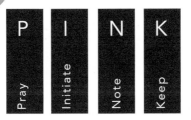

P — Pray
I — Initiate
N — Note
K — Keep

Be a good friend to yourself.
God loves you and wants you to
love yourself. Be kind to yourself,
and be patient as you learn and
grow. You're the one person you
can never get away from. You will
be a better friend to others when
you learn to treat yourself right.

Friendship with oneself is all-important, because without it one cannot be friends with anyone else in the world.

—Eleanor Roosevelt[vi]

3 friendship killers you must avoid

Good friends are hard to come by, and acquiring good friends is only half the battle. The other half is keeping them. If you want to keep your friends, I suggest you don't do these friendship killers.

1 Gossip.

Gossip is simply mischievous talk about the affairs of others. The Bible says that a gossip separates close friends. (Prov. 16:28.) A good friend will keep what he or she knows in confidence, unless someone in authority needs to be notified.

2 Selfishness.

How can we expect to keep the company of others if we are only concerned about ourselves? In Philippians 2:3, Paul wrote that we are to consider others better than ourselves. If we act unselfishly, we will encourage our friendships to grow.

Unforgiveness.

Our friends will make mistakes. Why? Because they are human. As our friends miss it and then turn from their mistakes or sin, we are to forgive them. We forgive our friends as Christ forgave us. (Eph. 4:31,32.)

no longer
lonely

Have you ever been lonely? Maybe you're lonely at this very moment. I want so much for you to not be. God created us as social beings with a need for one another. He doesn't want us to be lonely.

You may be that girl who has cried herself to sleep at night, and as you're reading this book about girlfriends, you're thinking, *Yeah, right. I don't even have one single friend. I don't belong anywhere.*

Can I tell you something? That's not God's will for any of us. He wants for us to know His love through His Son and also through others. Our desire to love and be loved was placed in us by our heavenly Father. He wants us to enjoy our lives, and a major part of that has to do with giving love to the Lord and others, as well as receiving love from the Lord and others.

Don't you ever give up on God's promises for you, and don't you dare put up with one more second of the god of this world (the devil) stealing, killing, and destroying your dreams for the wonderful friendships God has for you! The enemy loves to lie to us and make us feel so unworthy, rejected, unloved, unaccepted, and friendless. No more! No way!

Our Bible tells us that we are loved, accepted, worthy, valued, and cherished. When we recognize where these thoughts are coming from, we can win this battle. The enemy would love for us to isolate ourselves from everyone and make us think we have to be alone, that no one could ever understand what we're going through, that we are the only ones in the world facing the circumstances we might be in. He wants us to think, *No one has ever had the problems I have,* or *No one has ever messed up as bad as I have.* All I can say to that is, *What a lie!*

I am telling you the truth right now, and the truth will set you free! We need one another. We need our family and friends and our church family. These relationships are so important to all of us. If you're feeling any loneliness at all, I'd like to take this opportunity to pray for you.

Lord, I thank You for my dear friend—Your beloved daughter. Thank You for bringing friends into her life. Thank You for knitting her heart together with wonderful, godly women whom she can call her girlfriends. You know what a blessing these girls will be to her and how much they will benefit from her being in their lives.

I command all of these thoughts of inadequacy and words of rejection to be erased from her mind and her heart right now, in Jesus' name. She is clothed in Your love and acceptance. Thank You for reminding her every day that she is adopted by You, Lord. She is the apple of Your eye. She is engraved on the palm of Your hand. Nothing will ever separate her from Your love. You love her with perfect love, and Your perfect love casts out all fear. She will no longer be intimidated. Instead, she will begin to hold her head high and walk in the favor You have bestowed upon her. Thank You, Father, for being our most faithful friend ever and never leaving us alone. Thank You for answering our prayer.

think pink

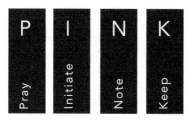

P — Pray
I — Initiate
N — Note
K — Keep

Say these words out loud:

GOD loves me. God LOVES me. God loves ME. I am God's daughter, and I have favor with Him and others. Thank You, Lord, for bringing true, loyal, godly friends into my life. I am a true, loyal, godly friend. God hasn't given me a spirit of fear. Instead, He has given me a spirit of love, power, and a sound mind. I am never alone. Father, You will never, never, never leave me or forsake me.

I love You, Lord, with all of my heart, mind, soul, and strength, and I love my neighbor as myself. Nothing will ever separate me from the love of God—absolutely nothing.

I will not be afraid to reach out to others who are lonely, because Your love is shed abroad in my heart by the Holy Spirit.

Thank You, Lord, for giving me courage to reach out to girls who are lonely. Use me to help heal broken hearts.

I will say what You say about me. The Word is very near me—in my mouth, in my mind, and in my heart—so I can do it. Thank You, Lord!

The glory of friendship is not the outstretched hand, nor the kindly smile, nor the joy of companionship; it is the spiritual inspiration that comes to one when you discover that someone else believes in you and is willing to trust you with a friendship.

—Ralph Waldo Emerson[vii]

if God had a refrigerator

If God had a refrigerator, your picture would be on it.

If He had a wallet, your photo would be in it.

He sends you flowers every spring and a sunrise every morning.

Whenever you want to talk, He'll listen.

He can live anywhere in the universe, and He chose your heart.

What about the Christmas gift He sent you in Bethlehem, not to mention that Friday at Calvary?

Face it, friend. He's crazy about you.

Author Unknown

5 attitudes that are friend magnets

There are always those people you are naturally attracted to, those friends you want to spend all of your free time with. What is it about those people that makes others want to be around them? Here are 5 character traits that make people "friend magnets."

1. Happiness.

Nobody wants to be around a grump. A great attitude is one of the strongest magnets for friends. When you are happy, it's contagious. Always try to stay upbeat, and you will never cease to be in the company of friends.

2. Encouragement.

Choosing to lift other people up with a kind word or a generous action will naturally draw other people to your side. A word in due season is often just the encouragement someone else needs. (Prov. 15:23.)

⭐ **3** *Generosity.*

Unselfishness is a powerfully attractive force. By choosing to share and to think of others before yourself, you show people that you value them.

⭐ **4.** *Objectiveness.*

It's nice to be around people who are willing to hear the opinions of others. Let's face it: You're not always right, so pick your battles carefully and be willing to accept someone else's idea if it's better than yours.

⭐ **5.** *Helpfulness.*

You're not much of a friend if you're not willing to lend a hand. It works both ways. There will be a time when you need some help, so sow the seeds of friendship now, and you will reap the rewards later.

5 surefire ways to make new friends in a new place

A new place can often be intimidating and lonely. But it can also be a great adventure if you take the initiative to meet new people. Even if you are naturally a shy person, if you follow these simple steps, you will find it easy to make new friends.

1. Take advantage of every opportunity to introduce yourself to people.

Introduce yourself to people in the school bookstore, cafeteria, library, and in class. The more people you meet, the greater the odds that you will find people you really connect with.

2. Remember to use people's names.

There is no better sound to a person than his or her own name. If you aren't good at remembering names, here is a little trick that will help. When you introduce yourself and your new acquaintance gives you their name, be sure to use it right away.

For example, "Sarah, it sure is good to meet you. Sarah, what classes do you have this semester?" If you can use their name at least three times in your conversation, you will be more likely to remember it. They will also be impressed the next time you see them and use their name.

3. Ask them questions about themselves.

Your conversation will be a hit because you are talking about their favorite subject—them! Everyone's favorite subject is themselves. It is often said, God gave us 2 ears and 1 mouth because He wants us to do twice as much listening as talking. A university study has found that good listening can be worth as much as 20 IQ points. I'll take all the extra points I can get!

4. Have good eye contact. If your eyes are always wandering during your conversation, people will feel you are uninterested in them.

Also, poor eye contact can send them the message that you are insecure or are hiding something from them.

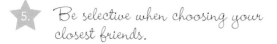

5. *Be selective when choosing your closest friends.*

Close friends are people who influence your values, self-esteem, and dreams. Be careful to choose friends who love God as you do, believe in your dreams, and build you up. If they are always tearing you down, you can do something about it: Get some new friends. A famous mathematician once said, "You have to have seven positives to overcome one negative." Life is too short to waste it with people who don't believe in you.

what the Bible has to say about friends

As iron sharpens iron, a friend sharpens a friend.

Proverbs 27:17 NLT

Anyone who loves a pure heart and gracious speech is the king's friend.

Proverbs 22:11 NLT

Do not be misled: "Bad company corrupts good character."

1 Corinthians 15:33 NIV

Keep away from angry, short-tempered people, or you will learn to be like them and endanger your soul.

Proverbs 22:24,25 NLT

A friend is always loyal, and a brother [or sister] is born to help in time of need.

Proverbs 17:17 NLT

You can trust a friend who corrects you, but kisses from an enemy are nothing but lies.

Proverbs 27:6 CEV

Whoever walks with the wise will become wise; whoever walks with fools will suffer harm.

Proverbs 13:20 NLT

When two of you get together on anything at all on earth and make a prayer of it, my Father in heaven goes into action.

Matthew 18:19 MSG

A friend loves at all times....

Proverbs 17:17 NIV

Love each other as brothers and sisters and honor others more than you do yourself.

Romans 12:10 CEV

Every good and perfect gift is from above.

James 1:17 NIV

Your task is to single-mindedly serve Christ. Do that and you'll kill two birds with one stone: pleasing the God above you and proving your worth to the people around you.

Romans 14:18 MSG

Make a careful exploration of who you are and the work you have been given, and then sink yourself into that. Don't be impressed with yourself. Don't compare yourself with others. Each of you must take responsibility for doing the creative best you can with your own life.

Galatians 6:4,5 MSG

every teen girl's
little pink book
on gab

*girls
about to
become*

Girls like to gab, and gab is great because all that talking is what makes you who you are! If what you think about, you talk about and bring about, then what you say is very important. You can make the most of your words in every situation. Talking and sharing with your friends and family is fun. Discover how to be heard, enjoyed, and respected for what you say and who you are!

the gift of gab

Have you ever heard the term "the gift of gab"? Gab isn't always a gift! But it can be when we use our mouths to bless. The Bible says that when we speak, we either speak life or death. Our words are containers of power for good or for evil! I want to use my mouth for good, and I know you do too.

Life and death are in the power of the tongue. I have to say, that is one powerful little muscle in our mouth, and we absolutely need to exercise control over it! Now, how do we do that?

Well, we need to ask the Lord to help us. For example, you can say, "Lord, help me to say good and kind words to everyone in my life."

Guess what? Included in that *everyone* is you! You have got to talk about yourself and to yourself in a good and kind way! You need to encourage your friends, your family, *and* yourself with God's Word.

A bit in the mouth of a horse controls the whole horse. A small rudder on a huge ship in the hands of a skilled captain sets a course in the face of the strongest winds. A word out of your mouth may seem of no account, but it can accomplish nearly anything—or destroy it! It only takes a spark, remember, to set off a forest fire.

James 3:3-5 MSG

Take charge! Think before you speak!

Now, let me be the first to tell you right here and now that I am so thankful to God for forgiveness. In the past, my gab has not always been good gab. We all have areas in our lives where we are growing and changing. When we confess our sin, our heavenly Father is so faithful to forgive us and give us a new beginning. He makes our sin-stained hearts as white as snow!

Our speech is something we will have to work on for the rest of our lives. We can't let our guard down. We've got to stay on our toes. We just need to daily ask the Lord for help to use our words wisely.

When I was about 11, 12, and 13 years old, I was a "cusser." I'm not proud to tell you that, but I share it with you for a reason. When I asked Jesus to come into my heart, it was like He took a bar of soap and washed my mouth out! One day I had some really bad gab coming out of my mouth; the next day it was gone! That made me so happy, and it was a very obvious change to my friends. I have never had a desire to cuss since.

I am so thankful I don't say those words anymore. That wouldn't be appropriate for a pastor's wife! Really, it's not attractive for any young woman to speak like that.

> Watch the way you talk. Let nothing foul or dirty come out of your mouth. Say only what helps, each word a gift. Don't grieve God. Don't break his heart. His Holy Spirit, moving and breathing in you, is the most intimate part of your life, making you fit for himself. Don't take such a gift for granted.

> *Ephesians 4:29,30 MSG*

This Scripture isn't just talking about cussing. I believe it's talking about gossiping, backbiting, telling dirty jokes, and even complaining.

Proverbs 16:28 says that gossip separates the best of friends. Don't you know that if you have a friend that is always gossiping about other people, there's a big chance she's talking about you when you're not around?

We all need to check up on ourselves and have a little mouth-washing ceremony once in a while. Just as we can whiten our teeth, we can whiten what comes out of our mouths!

If you are having trouble with your mouth, you can do these things to get it clean again.

Pray. The Lord will help you if you ask Him to.

Ask a friend to help you. Make yourself accountable to a friend. Tell your sins to each other, and pray for each other so you may be healed. "The prayer of a person living right with God is something powerful and to be reckoned with" (James 5:16 MSG).

Always trust the Lord to help you conquer bad habits and develop new habits in every area of your life. Say this: "I can do all things through Christ who strengthens me" (Phil. 4:13 NKJV).

think pink

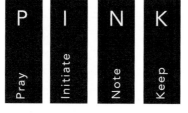

PROVERBS
15:1 NKJV

A soft answer turns away
wrath, but a harsh word
stirs up anger.

Conversation is an
exercise of the mind;
gossip is merely an
exercise of the tongue.

—Author Unknown

gossip

A false witness will not go unpunished, and he who speaks lies shall perish.

Proverbs 19:9 NKJV

A man gossiped about his friend. Soon his friend confronted him, and the gossiper became very sorrowful for the wrong he had done. He asked for his friend's forgiveness, which he granted, and asked if he could do anything to make things right between them. The friend said, "Take two down pillows and go to the center of town; cut the pillows open and wave them in the air till the feathers are all out. Then come back and see me."

The man did just as he'd been told and came back to his friend. The friend said, "I've forgiven you. But to realize how much harm your gossiping has caused me, go back to the center of town and collect all the feathers." The man regretfully realized it would be impossible to find and collect every feather.

Gossip hurts people, destroys relationships, and harms the gossiper. Gossiping causes people to distrust you. They are thinking in the back of their minds, *If she gossips about this person behind her back, what is she saying about me behind mine?* Respect yourself and others: Don't gossip.

details, details

Girls are detailed. We love to know exactly what happened when our best friend got her driver's license or when she had her hair done. And we want to tell every detail when something happens to us.

The benefit of all those thoughts and details is that we consider all the aspects of a problem before we decide on a solution. The negative is that we sometimes have trouble deciding what to do because we are considering so much information. You've probably heard the saying, "It's a girl's prerogative to change her mind," and that's right because we have so many different options!

The challenge is keeping our foot out of our mouth and staying focused. We are so tempted to just blurt out those thoughts before considering what we are going to say.

Proverbs shows us that when we hold our tongue we are wise.

When words are many, sin is not absent,
but he who holds his tongue is wise.

Proverbs 10:19 NIV

We can all learn from that one, huh? Think of a time recently when you wish you would have held your tongue. Would you have been seen as wise instead of foolish?

think pink

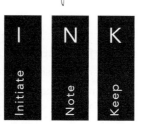

PROVERBS 21:9 AMP

a girl no one wants to marry
(or even date!)

It is better to dwell in a corner of the
housetop [on the flat oriental roof,
exposed to all kinds of weather] than
in a house shared with a nagging,
quarrelsome, and faultfinding woman.

The best way to
cheer yourself is
to try to cheer
someone else up.

—Mark Twain[ii]

6 gabs to avoid

We have all been in relationships in which we thought someone was our true friend and then down the road realized she wasn't. A true friend doesn't just call herself a friend, but backs up her words with action. Check out the gab from these 6 so-called "friends," and learn to avoid them.

1. Backstabber

This is someone who talks one way in front of you, but says something totally different behind your back. A backstabber cannot be trusted by anyone.

2. User

The user is just looking for a temporary friend. This person will sweet-talk you for personal gain and then toss you out like a dirty dishrag.

3. Control freak

"It's my way or the highway," this one will say. The control freak will not compromise. You're only going and doing what this person wants to do. Your opinion doesn't matter.

⭐ 4. Manipulator

If you don't want to do what the manipulator wants you to do, this person will find a way to convince you to do it her way. The manipulator is sly and will influence you to do things you never thought you would do—all for her own selfish ambitions.

⭐ 5. Moocher

This person wants you to provide for her every need. "Can I borrow your clothes?" "Can I borrow your car?" "Can I borrow a couple of bucks?" As you give, you'll never receive anything in return.

⭐ 6. Complainer

You can never please the complainer no matter what you do. If you gave this person a $100 bill, she would complain because it's not two $50 bills. Save yourself, and avoid this one.

gab test

Gab can be a curse or a gift, depending on how we choose to use it. When we say the right thing at the right time, our words can actually soothe people and bring healing. Good and kind words can change someone's life.

Let's take a moment and do a little heart checkup. Be very honest with yourself as you go through these questions.

1. *Am I a **blabber gabber**?*

Definition: One who gossips and spreads rumors, always saying something negative about her family and friends.

Yes   No   Sometimes

2. *Am I a **crabby gabby**?*

Definition: One who is constantly grumbling and complaining about everything. One who is mad at the world, bent out of shape, bitter, and cranky.

Yes   No   Sometimes

3   *Am I a **drab gab**?*

Definition: One who is always talking about negative, depressing things. One who sees the glass half-empty and sounds a lot like Eeyore.

Yes   No   Sometimes

4   *Am I a **jab gab**?*

Definition: One who continually pokes fun at people. One who feels better about oneself by making fun of people.

Yes   No   Sometimes

5.   *Am I a **stab gab**? Ouch!*

Definition: One who stabs people in the back with words. Very "mean girls" do this!

It's brutal, dangerous, hurts a lot, and is very deceptive!

Yes   No   Sometimes

⭐ 6   *Am I a **tabs gab**?*

Definition: One who puts her nose in everyone's business. One who feels it is her responsibility to keep tabs on everyone and let everyone else know about it. Also known as a busybody gab.

Yes   No   Sometimes

⭐ 7   *Am I a **fab gab**?*

Definition: One who uses gab to encourage, build up, give life, kindness, and wisdom. This is delightful, beautiful, and extremely pleasing!

Yes   Yes   Yes

think pink

P — Pray
I — Initiate
N — Note
K — Keep

1 THESSALONIANS
5 : 14 MSG

Gently encourage the stragglers,
and reach out for the exhausted,
pulling them to their feet.
Be patient with each person,
attentive to individual needs.

"Watch your thoughts; they become your words. Watch your words; they become your actions. Watch your actions; they become your habits. Watch your habits; they become your character. Watch your character for it will become your destiny."

—Frank Outlaw[iii]

gabsters

Most girls like to talk a lot, and God made us that way on purpose. We're gabsters! We think with both sides of our brain, so we have lots of thoughts: some creative, some logical, some that make sense, and some that don't! With all those thoughts rolling around in our heads, it's easy to speak out. That can help us or can work against us. Let me share with you some great ways to let those words work for you.

> Death and life are in the power of the tongue, and they who indulge in it shall eat the fruit of it [for death or life].
>
> *Proverbs 18:21 AMP*

We can speak good things out of our mouths and, as a result, enjoy good things in our lives. But if we speak negative things, we can generate negative results in our lives.

Who would think that words could affect your life so much? But it's true. Your words count. Make it a habit to *speak life*. Speak good things. Sometimes that's hard, especially when you are faced with a difficult circumstance. You might want to just complain or cry, but if you can find a positive Scripture to say in that situation instead, you will be on the path to success.

Here's one Scripture to keep in your memory next time you feel overwhelmed.

> You, dear children, are from God and have overcome them, because the one who is in you is greater than the one who is in the world.
>
> 1 John 4:4 NIV

Let God's Word be your motto in tough times, and enjoy the benefits of good words!

think pink

P R O V E R B S
2 5 : 1 1   A M P

A word fitly spoken and in
due season is like apples of
gold in settings of silver.

The reason a dog has so many friends is that he wags his tail instead of his tongue.

—Author Unknown

lift

Do not be deceived, God is not mocked; for whatever a man sows, that he will also reap.

Galatians 6:7 NKJV

Look at some of these creative cut-downs, and see if you have ever been guilty of using them:

 "You got into the gene pool when the lifeguard wasn't watching."

 "If I gave you a penny for your thoughts, you'd get change."

"When you open your mouth, it's only to change whatever foot was previously in there."

Small people cut others down to feel good about themselves. A person with a healthy self-esteem doesn't need to.

If you want to feel good, help someone else feel good. Reach out. Be a friend. Give a kind word. Be the bigger person: Lift others up to your level rather than cutting them down.

chatty cathy

When I was a little girl, I had a doll named Chatty Cathy. (She's sold in antique stores now. Ouch!) Anyway, I would pull her string and she would "chat": "Hi, I'm Chatty Cathy. How are you today? I love you!" and so on. My mom told me that I went through a couple of those dolls because I would wear them right out.

I guess most of us girls need to get control of *our* string and give *our* voice a rest, so we don't wear ourselves and others out!

When my husband is watching something on TV (usually a football or hockey game) and doesn't want to be disturbed, he's been known to try to mute me with the remote when I try to chat. That's not very nice, is it?

But it really is something to think about. We really can't mute ourselves with an electronic device. Therefore, our only option is self-control, not a remote control!

think pink

P Pray

I Initiate

N Note

K Keep

PSALM 141 : 3 , 4 MSG

Post a guard at my mouth,
God, set a watch at the door of
my lips. Don't let me so much
as dream of evil or thoughtlessly
fall into bad company. And
these people who only do
wrong—don't let them lure me
with their sweet talk!

chatty cathy

There are people who, instead of listening to what is being said to them, are already listening to what they are going to say themselves.

—Albert Guinon[iv]

control

For in many things we offend all. If any man offend not in word, the same is a perfect man, and able also to bridle the whole body.

James 3:2

This verse says that by controlling the tongue, we are able to control the desires and impulses of the entire body.

We live in a body that has fleshly desires and wants to commit stupid sins. The way we will be able to control these desires is by speaking the right words. If we talk about sex all the time, guess what we're going to do really soon?

Our words will guide and direct our life, so we need to weigh each one carefully and let the Word of God be a regular part of our vocabulary.

2 ears—
1 mouth

Have you ever noticed that when we girls get together, we can talk so fast and furious? We are known for this.

Sometimes when I'm with a group of ladies and we're just visiting, someone may tell a story that triggers a story that I want to tell. I find myself just wanting to get my turn in. I have had to tell myself, "Calm down, Cathy. Don't be rude." I hate when I have interrupted someone out of just plain rudeness.

We all like to get our 2 cents in. It's so much fun to get together with our friends, but we really have to remember to bring our manners with us.

When my boys were little and we were going somewhere, I'd say right before we'd get out of the car, "Did you bring your manners? Okay, let's put them on!"

Have you ever left somewhere and just kicked yourself all the way home because you got carried away in your conversation? I've done that, and I'm very thankful for God's forgiveness. I've learned that I sure save myself a lot of trouble when I think before I speak.

We need to keep this Scripture in our hearts and do it:

> Don't think only about your own affairs, but be interested in others, too, and what they are doing.
>
> *Philippians 2:4 NLT*

Remember: 2 ears, 1 mouth. God gave us 2 ears so we could listen twice as much as we speak. We'll be amazed at how much we can learn if we just make a point to listen once in a while. This takes practice if we're not used to it, but I know we can all learn to be good listeners.

think pink

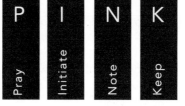

P — Pray
I — Initiate
N — Note
K — Keep

PROVERBS
17:28 NKJV

*Even a fool is counted wise when he
holds his peace; when he shuts his lips,
he is considered perceptive.*

Men are born with two
eyes, but only one tongue,
in order that they should
see twice as much
as they say.

—Charles Caleb Colton[v]

listen up

A great American leadership and management trainer recently said, "In hundreds of interviews with people at all levels, I've made this discovery: The bigger the person, the more apt he is to encourage you to talk; the smaller the person, the more apt he is to preach to you. Big people monopolize the listening; small people monopolize the talking!"

There's a reason God gave us 2 ears and 1 mouth. Good leaders are great listeners, as are good friends. Are you more concerned with hearing or being heard?

guys

God put it in you to be attracted to guys. Just don't go overboard in your thoughts and words. Guys aren't every-thing (even though they may seem to be). The guys you know today might not even cross your mind in 2 or 3 years. Hold out for God's best. Don't commit too much.

After Eve was deceived by Satan in the Garden of Eden, the Lord said to her, "Your desire will be for your husband, and he will rule over you" (Gen. 3:16 NIV). Since that desire is in you, keep tabs on it. You can control your thoughts and emotions and save the best for the man you marry.

friends

Proverbs 18:24 NLT says, "There are 'friends' who destroy each other, but a real friend sticks closer than a brother."

A true friend sticks closer than a brother or sister. That means true friends don't slice and dice each other with their words. Maybe you and your friends tore each other down in fourth grade, but now you're making friends for life. Words can hurt, or words can heal. When you have friends, you stick by each other—especially with your words.

teachers

Seems like you either love them or, uh, are challenged with them. You can find favor with either kind of teacher—even the most difficult one. If you say positive things over your relationships with teachers and keep yourself from talking them down with your friends, you can build favor for yourself. It might be tough to keep it quiet, especially when you'd like to rip those teachers to shreds, but you will win in the long run if you keep the trash talk out of your life.

> Let not mercy and truth forsake you; bind them around your neck, write them on the tablet of your heart, and so find favor and high esteem in the sight of God and man.
>
> Proverbs 3:3,4 NKJV

You can place "teacher" in that verse instead of "man." What teacher can you pray that Scripture over? I do it like this:

> *Father God, I thank You that I am merciful and truthful and that I have favor in Your sight and with my teachers, in Jesus' name.*

parents

The Word of God tells us that we should honor our parents. Of the Ten Commandments, it's the first one with a promise. That promise is a long life!

> Children, obey your parents in the Lord, for this is right. "Honor your father and mother," which is the first command-ment with promise: "that it may be well with you and you may live long on the earth."
>
> *Ephesians 6:1-3 NKJV*

How do you honor your parents? Is it just doing what they say? Actually, that word "honor" in the *Amplified Bible* version is to "esteem and value as precious." That means your attitude matters too. You honor them by keeping a good attitude even when you don't want to. A good attitude includes saying good words about them. You can do it! It's worth a long life, and you'll win big points with your parents and God.

think pink

PINK

Pray

Initiate

Note

Keep

COLOSSIANS
| 4 : 6 NIV

*Let your conversation be
always full of grace, seasoned
with salt, so that you may
know how to answer everyone.*

Always attempt to be mannerly and gracious, seeking never to offend in word or deed, always considering the feelings of others.

—Sharon Daugherty[vi]

If you can't say something nice, don't say nothing at all!

—Thumper

3 things to gab with your parents

Communication is the key to victory in any kind of relationship. Great companies, great armies, great churches, great sports teams, and great homes all have 1 thing in common: They have learned to communicate effectively with one another. Communication is not just talking. It is listening, observing, studying, and, finally, talking. People who only learn to talk are not communicating; they are spewing. In opening up good communication lines with your parents, there are 3 things you must always tell them.

★ 1 *Tell them when you need help.*

It may be in school, a relationship, or a job, but if you need help and guidance, let your parents know. That's why God gave them to you: to help you get through tough times.

2. *Tell them when you've made a mistake.*

It might be easier at the time to try to cover it up. However, honesty not only will help you avoid making this same mistake again; it will also earn you big points in the "trust" quest.

3. *Tell them you love and appreciate them.*

Sure, there's no such thing as a perfect parent, but most all have made a very significant investment of time, energy, and money in their children. Regularly let yours know you love them, even if they don't always show the same love in return.

good gab
(the best gab of all)

There is one type of gab that is in a category of its own. It's the kind of gab that we can only experience with God, and it is the most powerful thing we can do with our mouths. When we talk with God and thank Him, and when we remind Him of His words to us, our mouths are being used to accomplish His will in this world.

As we spend time with Jesus, it will be very evident to others that we've been in His presence by how we speak.

For example:

> When we take time to worship the Lord and thank Him for all He's doing in our lives, our conversations with others begin to show that we have a thankful heart. "I will bless the Lord at all times; His praise will continually come out of my mouth" (Ps. 34:1).

> When we cast our cares on the Lord, as He has asked us to, our words will be full of faith

and confidence rather than dread and worry. Our help comes from the Lord, and when we give our care to Him we are assured that He will take care of us. (Ps. 121:2; 1 Peter 5:7.)

When we ask for forgiveness (a very important part of prayer), we are forgiven! The Bible says that when we confess (with our mouths) our sins, God is faithful and just to forgive us and to cleanse us from all unrighteousness. That means we are in right standing with Him. That sin is washed away. When we receive forgiveness, we are able to hold our heads up and, therefore, able to look into other people's eyes and speak to them of God's love and mercy. Our words will bring joy and peace to people in our lives.

The Lord has called us as His daughters to stand in the gap for others. What a privilege to pray for others to receive salvation! Now, that is the most wonderful way to make ourselves and our mouths available to God.

Prayer heals broken hearts, sets people free from addictions, opens people's eyes to the truth, and makes them whole in their spirit, soul, and body.

I'm so thankful for the people who have prayed for you and me and our loved ones. Let's always be thoughtful and ready to pray for others.

think pink

PROVERBS 16:23

I think before I speak
because the mind of the wise
instructs her mouth.

A slip of the foot you may soon recover, but a slip of the tongue you may never get over.

—Benjamin Franklin[vii]

meditate

Let the words of my mouth, and the meditation of my heart, be acceptable in thy sight, O Lord, my strength, and my redeemer.

Psalm 19:14

This Scripture ties the words of our mouths to the meditations of our hearts. See, whatever we think about is what we're going to be talking about with our mouths. Of course, there are always a few in every crowd who fail to think at all before they talk, but for the most part our mouths follow our thoughts.

When someone talks about meditation, the image that usually surfaces in our minds is a Chinese-looking guy in a toga, sitting cross-legged, his eyes closed and his fingers in circles, humming in G minor. (At least it does in my imagination.)

However, to His eternal credit, this is not what God has in mind when He tells us to meditate. He's simply asking us to take a few extra moments in our day to really think about and mull over His Word.

When you do, you'll gain new revelation and better understanding about how to make it work in your life.

C'mon—try it.

believe in your gab

Another word to describe a "Christian," or follower of Jesus Christ, is "believer." We should be called "believers" because we believe that Jesus Christ is the Son of God and have accepted Him as our Lord. Believers believe. It's important that we believe in what we say, just as we believe in Jesus Christ. Jesus tells us this in the book of Mark.

> "For assuredly, I say to you, whoever says to this mountain, 'Be removed and be cast into the sea,' and does not doubt in his heart, but believes that those things he says will be done, he will have whatever he says. Therefore I say to you, whatever things you ask when you pray, believe that you receive them, and you will have them."
>
> *Mark 11:23,24 NKJV*

When we pray, if we believe that we receive what we ask for, Jesus says we will indeed receive them. But if you say things that are not true most of time, then when it comes time to pray, it's pretty tough to believe that you'll get what you ask for. When your words are messed up, your believer is all messed up! Your spiritual side doesn't know when to believe or when not to believe.

Have you ever known someone who just seemed to lie about everything? You couldn't trust them. It's the same with your spiritual side. If you mix up your words with some truth and some other stuff, you can't trust yourself when you pray. Remember the quote from Shakespeare's play *Hamlet:* "To thine own self be true."

In the book of Hebrews, the writer tells us that the children of Israel did not enter the Promised Land because they had an unbelieving heart. (Heb. 3:7-12.) Don't let an unbelieving heart stop you from receiving God's best. If you ask the Lord to help you, He'll let you know on the inside when you've crossed over the line of unbelief with your words. Then you can correct it right then. That will keep your believer strong!

think pink

P — Pray
I — Initiate
N — Note
K — Keep

HEBREWS 4:14 NKJV

Seeing then that we have a great High Priest who has passed through the heavens, Jesus the Son of God, let us hold fast our confession.

Father God, I am a believer and stand strong in my declaration of faith. You are my very present help in trouble. You guide me and lead me into all truth. You cause my thoughts to become agreeable to Your will, and so my plans are established and succeed, in Jesus' name. Amen.

believe in your gab

Wise men speak because they have something to say; Fools because they have to say something.

—Plato[viii]

3 things to erase from your thoughts and gab

The Bible teaches us in 2 Corinthians 10:5 to cast down every high thought that would try to exalt itself against the knowledge of God. The act of casting down must be aggressive, and it must be followed with intentionally thinking what will encourage your walk with Christ. Guard carefully against the following thoughts, because they turn into words.

1 "No one cares about you."

This thought tempts us towards self-pity, but it is a lie. People do care and, most importantly, God cares! Say out loud, "God cares about me, and people care about me."

2 "You won't succeed."

You have every reason to be confident of success if you are walking with God. Philippians 4:13 says you can do all things though Christ who strengthens you. Say out loud, "I will succeed in life. Jesus Christ strengthens my spirit, soul, and body."

Just give up."

Jesus didn't quit on you. He doesn't have a quitting spirit, and He didn't put a quitting spirit in you. Persevere and finish the race! Say out loud, "I will not quit. I have a strong spirit. I will find my destiny, and I will finish my course."

get what you gab

The same way you received Jesus as your Lord is the same way you receive all things from God. You say, "Jesus, come into my life. I believe You are the Son of God and that You died for my sins and rose again." You find this in the book of Romans:

> That if you confess with your mouth, "Jesus is Lord," and believe in your heart that God raised him from the dead, you will be saved. For it is with your heart that you believe and are justified, and it is with your mouth that you confess and are saved.
>
> *Romans 10:9,10 NIV*

This principle of believing with your heart and saying with your mouth is how you receive from God. If you are sick and need to be healed, you can find a Scripture in the Bible that says you are healed. For instance, 1 Peter 2:24 says that by the stripes of Jesus you are healed. You believe that Scripture is true for you, and then you say that Scripture over your life. Words and thoughts are important to God. He made an easy way for you to connect with Him and change the circumstances in your life: talk!

think pink

P Pray
I Initiate
N Note
K Keep

HEBREWS 11:3 NLV

Through faith we understand that the world was made by the Word of God. Things we see were made from what could not be seen.

When God created the world, He used words. When He spoke, things happened. God said, "Let there be light," and light was. God said, "Let the earth bring forth living creatures," and animals appeared. His words caused the science of this world to form.

In the same way, your words can affect your world. Keep your words positive, and speak life!

Just as God created the world with words, you and I can create our world around us by the words of our mouth.

—Kate McVeigh[ix]

7 words to remove from your gab

1. *"Can't."*

You can do all things through Christ who strengthens you. (Phil. 4:13.)

2. *"Never."*

All things are possible to those who believe. (Mark 9:23.)

3. *"Quit."*

"Let us not grow weary while doing good, for in due season we shall reap if we do not lose heart" (Gal. 6:9 NKJV).

4. *"Depressed."*

"Rejoice in the Lord always: and again I say, Rejoice" (Phil. 4:4).

5. *"Hate."*

The Holy Ghost sheds the love of God abroad in our hearts. (Rom. 5:5.)

6. *"Doubt."*

"So then faith comes by hearing, and hearing by the word of God" (Rom. 10:17 NKJV).

7. *"Broke."*

My God shall supply all of your needs by His riches in glory in Christ Jesus. (Phil. 4:19.)

kind gab

Psalm 45:1 says that our tongue is as the pen of a ready writer. The book of Proverbs says we are to write God's Word on the tablet of our hearts. Let's use our tongues to write God's love on people's hearts.

In Proverbs 31, the Bible tells us about a woman who is very wise. It says that when she speaks, she always has something worthwhile to say and she always says it kindly. When she opens her mouth she shares wisdom, and the law of kindness is on her tongue. I just want to encourage you that you are very capable of being that young Proverbs 31 woman.

If you haven't taken charge of your tongue, begin right now. There is no telling how many lives you can help and bless by speaking life-giving words. The bottom line is that our words help bring people closer to the Lord.

We have good news to share with people. We can't leave it all up to the preachers. There are people who won't give any preacher the time of day, but will listen to your testimony. There are people who won't otherwise step foot in a church, but will one day to hear your pastor or youth pastor because you opened your mouth and lovingly invited them to come with you. The next thing you know, they will have received Jesus into their hearts because you reached out with a wise and kind word. I'd say that's using your gab as a gift! The best gift of all—salvation!

Proverbs 11:30 says the fruit of those who are right with God is a tree of life, and he who wins souls is wise!

think pink

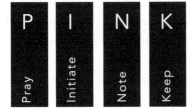

Make an effort today to minister
words of life to a friend.

There are many men whose tongues might govern multitudes if they could govern their tongues.

—George D. Prentice[x]

3 things God hates

There are six things the Lord hates, seven that are detestable to him: haughty eyes, a lying tongue, hands that shed innocent blood, a heart that devises wicked schemes, feet that are quick to rush into evil, a false witness who pours out lies and a man who stirs up dissension among brothers.

Proverbs 6:16-19

Notice that 3 of the 7 things the Lord hates have to do with our mouths.

God says He hates:

A lying tongue. We should ALWAYS speak the truth.

A false witness who pours out lies. God's daughters shouldn't lie about others. We don't want anyone lying about us, right?

A person who sows discord among brothers and sisters. In other words, mind your own business.

Wow! If we know how much the Lord loves us and we know He's given us these warnings for our protection, then we must take heed and ask Him to help us keep our tongue under control. As His girls, our words should be containers of truth and love.

The Lord simply doesn't like gossip. We shouldn't be spreading lies or negative things about others, even if it's true. We always want to help people up, not bring them down.

listen
before you
gab

Many times, the best preaching and teaching that Christ did was a direct result of listening to someone. People would come to Him with sometimes simple, and other times very difficult, questions. The Holy Spirit would give Jesus the answer every time. James 1:19 tells us to "be quick to listen, slow to speak." A listening heart attracts many friends and will always be rewarded with wisdom from heaven. Here are 4 reasons to have a listening heart.

1. Listening gives you time to fully evaluate a person's situation before you pass on counsel or advice that is premature.

2. Listening tells the person you care. It says that person is important and you are not in a rush to send them away.

3. Listening gives you time to hear from God. The Lord will speak to you clearly when you take unselfish interest in the lives of others.

God believes in listening. What do you think He's doing when we pray? He's listening. That's why He gave us 2 ears and 1 mouth: We ought to listen twice as much as we talk.

think pink

P I N K

Pray   Initiate   Note   Keep

PROVERBS
12:15 NLT

Fools think they need no advice,
but the wise listen to others.

Perhaps the most important thing we ever give each other is our attention.... A loving silence often has more power to heal and connect than the most well-intentioned words.

—Rachel Naomi Remen[xi]

3 secrets of a good listener

The Bible says that we are to "be quick to listen, slow to speak" (James 1:19 NIV). Unfortunately, many people are just the opposite and are very quick to speak and extremely slow to listen. When you take the time to listen to somebody, you are showing them that you care and have respect for what they think. It will cement your relationship with that person. What does it take to be a good listener? Here are 3 secrets.

1. Look into the eyes of the person you are listening to. This, more than anything, says, "I really do care about what you have to say."

2. Think about the point or concern they are sharing. Don't be rehearsing in your mind your answer before you've fully caught all that they are communicating.

3. Repeat back a brief synopsis of what they just told you. For example, "Jill, I know you feel sad about not making the team. I believe in you, and if you keep working at it, I think you'll make it next time."

gab with God

Matthew 4:4
NLV says:

But Jesus said, "It is written, 'Man is not to live on bread only. Man is to live by every word that God speaks.'"

God speaks. He gabs, and He created you to gab, too—especially with Him. He knew you before the foundations of the earth. He planned your life in advance.

Ephesians 2:10 AMP says,

For we are God's [own] handiwork (His workmanship), recreated in Christ Jesus, [born anew] that we may do those good works which God predestined (planned beforehand) for us [taking paths which He prepared ahead of time], that we should walk in them [living the good life which He prearranged and made ready for us to live].

God has a specific plan for you. When He speaks to you, take note of it. It may not happen immediately, but when it does, you'll be ready.

If you need direction from God, you can pray this:

Lord, my heart seeks You. I want to do the things that You have already planned for me to do. I'm ready to follow You. I'm waiting to hear Your direction for my life. I want Your best, in Jesus' name.

think pink

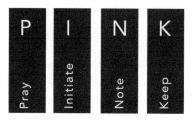

Write down the times when you heard God's direction and followed it. What was the outcome? How did you know it was the Lord? It's good to remember the times you heard from God. He is always ready to talk with you.

No heart thrives without much secret converse with God and nothing will make amends for the want of it.

—John Berridge[xii]

listening to God

However, I (Jesus) am telling you
nothing but the truth when I say it is
profitable (good, expedient, advanta-
geous) for you that I go away. Because
if I do not go away, the Comforter
(Counselor, Helper, Advocate, Inter-
cessor, Strengthener, Standby) will
not come to you [into close fellowship
with you]; but if I go away, I will send
Him to you [to be in close fellowship
with you.]

John 16:7 AMP

Jesus sent the Holy Spirit to fellowship with you.
That means he wants to listen to you, answer
your questions, give you direction, and help you.
But it is tough to receive help from the Lord
unless part of your prayer time is spent listening
to Him. He wants to tell you specific things about
what you are dealing with right now and what is
coming in your future. Remember: Anything the
Holy Spirit tells you will line up with what the
Bible says.

If you want to receive help from the Lord, you can pray this prayer:

> *Father God, thank You for sending the Holy Spirit to be my counselor and my friend. Help me to make time to listen for Your leading and to follow Your direction, in Jesus' name. Amen.*

gab goop

Have you ever made a mess with your gab and had to be forgiven? When your words get you in trouble, God made a way for you to be forgiven and in right standing with Him again.

But if we confess our sins to him, he is faithful and just to forgive us and cleanse us from every wrong.

1 John 1:9 NLT

Everyone makes mistakes and God is so good to have given you a way to receive freedom. This verse was not written to sinners; it was written to Christians. Just because you are saved does not mean you're perfect. God's mercy is here for you right now.

If your gab has made a mess, you can pray this prayer:

Father God, I'm sorry. Forgive me. Thank You for making me clean. Help me to start fresh, in Jesus' name.

think pink

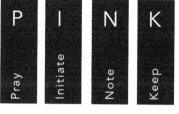

P — Pray
I — Initiate
N — Note
K — Keep

JAMES 4:8 MSG

Say a quiet yes to God and
he'll be there in no time.
Quit dabbling in sin.
Purify your inner life.
Quit playing the field.

Prayer is the great engine to overthrow and rout my spiritual enemies, the great means to procure the graces of which I stand in hourly need.

—John Newton[xiii]

courageous gab

The most courageous thing you can do as you become who you are destined to be is to remain faithful to God. As long as you are okay with God, you are okay with everything else. He is your sounding board. Bounce everything off of Him and get His feedback.

Second Timothy 2:11-13 NKJV says:

> This is a faithful saying: For if we died with Him, we shall also live with Him. If we endure, we shall also reign with Him. If we deny Him, He also will deny us. If we are faithless, He remains faithful; He cannot deny Himself.

People may not always be faithful to you, especially with their words, but God and His Word remain faithful forever.

think pink

P — Pray
I — Initiate
N — Note
K — Keep

PROVERBS 11 : 30 NLT

The godly are like trees that
bear life-giving fruit, and those
who save lives are wise.

"The very man who has argued you down, will sometimes be found, years later, to have been influenced by what you said."

—C.S. Lewis[xiv]

gab about God

As you grow in your relationship with God, your life will begin to reflect His goodness. Your gab will be filled with thoughts about Him and stories about His faithfulness in your life.

As you gab about God, some people won't want to listen. Some may even try to argue with you. Just remember that you aren't fighting with people; you are fighting the enemy of their souls. (Eph. 6:12.) Pray that God will open doors for you to share His goodness, that He will give you favor in every conversation, and that your friends' spiritual eyes will be opened to the truth.

As you plant word seeds into their lives and pray for them, God will send other believers to water the seeds—and one day you will see the reward of your work when your friends are worshipping God with their lives and words, too.

God bless you and your mouth. I believe with all of my heart that you will use your gab for good!

recommended reading

A Young Woman After God's Own Heart •
by Elizabeth George

Girl Talk • by Sheri Rose Shepherd

Girls Of Grace • by Point of Grace

Teenagers Are People Too • by Joyce Meyer

Little Black Books • by Blaine Bartel

For Such a Time as This • by Lisa Ryan

endnotes

every teen girl's little pink book

i   http://www.m-w.com/dictionary, s.v. "delight."

ii http://www.wow4u.com/daughters/index.html

iii http://www.m-w.com/dictionary, s.v. "aspire."

iv http://www.zaadz.com/quotes/topics/daughters?
    page=5

v   http://www.m-w.com/dictionary, s.v. "unashamed."

vi http://www.zaadz.com/quotes

vii http://www.m-w.com/dictionary, s.v. "generous."

viii http://www.m-w.com/dictionary, s.v. "honor."

ix http://www.coolquotes.com/honor.html

x   http://www.m-w.com/dictionary, s.v. "thankful."

xi http://www.zaadz.com/quotes/topics/thankfulness/?
    page=2

xii http://www.m-w.com/dictionary, s.v. "encourage."

xiii http://www.kindacts.org/quotes.cfm

xiv http://www.m-w.com/dictionary, s.v. "relationship."

xv http://www.zaadz.com/quotes/search?page=1&
    search=Relationships

little pink book for girlfriends

i   http://www.quotegarden.com/sisters.html

ii http://www.friendship.com.au/quotes/quohis.html

iii http://www.scrapbook.com/quotes/doc/3770/26.
    html

iv http://www.indianchild.com/friendship_quotations.html

v http://www.friendship.com.au/quotes/quofri.htmlell

vi http://www.friendship.com.au/quotes/quohis.html

vii http://www.coolquotes.com/searchresults.php?pageNum_RSAuthor=2&totalRows_RSAuthor=57&txtkeyword=friendship

little pink book on gab

i http://www.quotationspage.com/quote/8544.html

ii http://www.quotationspage.com/quote/26320.html

iii http://en.thinkexist.com/quotes/frank_outlaw/

iv http://www.quotationspage.com/quote/27741.html

v http://www.quotationspage.com/quote/2192.html

vi Walking in the Fruit of the Spirit (Tulsa: Victory Christian Center, 1998).

vii http://www.quotationspage.com/quote/34290.html

viii http://en.thinkexist.com/quotation/wise_men_speak_because_they_have_something_to_say/218003.html

ix Single and Loving It (Tulsa: Harrison House Publishers, 2003) p. 86.

x http://www.quotationspage.com/quote/9500.html

xi http://www.wisdomquotes.com/002329.html

xii http://www.cybernation.com/quotationcenter/quoteshow.php?type=author&id=845

xiii http://www.cybernation.com/quotationcenter/quoteshow.php?id=32289

xiv http://en.thinkexist.com/quotes/c.s._lewis/

prayer of salvation

God loves you—no matter who you are, no matter what your past. God loves you so much that He gave His one and only begotten Son for you. The Bible tells us that "...whoever believes in him shall not perish but have eternal life" (John 3:16 niv). Jesus laid down His life and rose again so that we could spend eternity with Him in heaven and experience His absolute best on earth. If you would like to receive Jesus into your life, say the following prayer out loud and mean it from your heart.

Heavenly Father, I come to You admitting that I am a sinner. Right now, I choose to turn away from sin, and I ask You to cleanse me of all unrighteousness. I believe that Your Son, Jesus, died on the cross to take away my sins. I also believe that He rose again from the dead so that I might be forgiven of my sins and made righteous through faith in Him. I call upon the name of Jesus Christ to be the Savior and Lord of my life. Jesus, I choose to follow You and ask that You fill me with the power of the Holy Spirit. I declare that right now I am a child of God. I am free from sin and full of the righteousness of God. I am saved in Jesus' name. Amen.

If you prayed this prayer to receive Jesus Christ as your Savior for the first time, please contact us on the Web at **www.harrisonhouse.com** to receive a free book.

Or you may write to us at
Harrison House
P.O. Box 35035
Tulsa, Oklahoma 74153

about the author

For more than a quarter of a century, Cathy Bartel has served alongside her husband, Blaine, in what they believe is the hope of the world, the local church. For the better part of two decades, they have served their pastor, Willie George, in building one of America's most respected churches, Church on the Move, in Tulsa, Oklahoma. Most recently, they helped found Oneighty, which has become one of the most emulated youth ministries in the past 10 years, reaching 2,500–3,000 students weekly under their leadership.

While Blaine is known for his communication and leadership skills, Cathy is known for her heart and hospitality. Blaine is quick to recognize her "behind the scenes" gifting to lift and encourage people as one of the great strengths of their ministry together. Her effervescent spirit and contagious smile open the door for her ministry each day, whether she's in the church or at the grocery store.

Cathy is currently helping Blaine raise a new community of believers committed to relevant ministry and evangelism. Northstar Church will open its doors in the growing north Dallas suburb of Frisco, Texas, in the fall of 2006.

Cathy's greatest reward has come in the raising of her 3 boys—Jeremy, 21, Dillon, 19, and Brock, 17. Today, each son is serving Christ with his unique abilities and is deeply involved in Blaine and Cathy's ongoing ministry.

To contact Cathy Bartel please write to:
Serving America's Future
P.O. Box 691923
Tulsa, Oklahoma 74169
www.blainebartel.com

*Please include your prayer requests
and comments when you write.*

every teen girl's

little pink book

on what to wear

by cathy bartel

God ideas for a great wardrobe

find out what's hot:

cool clothes

faith

smiles

beauty inside

modesty

God's love

fashion sense. personal style. get them both.

Available at fine bookstores everywhere or at **www.harrisonhouse.com**.

Harrison House

ISBN: 1-57794-795-9

every teenager's
little black book
special gift edition

by blaine bartel

answers
every teen
needs

You'll discover:

1. cool—be popular without losing your reputation

2. dating—be the right person, find the right person

3. dream—plan big, believe big

4. find—your place to belong

ISBN-10: 1-57794-908-0,

ISBN-13: 978-1-57794-908-4

Available at fine bookstores everywhere or at **www.harrisonhouse.com**.

the harrison house vision

Proclaiming the truth and the power

Of the Gospel of Jesus Christ

With excellence;

Challenging Christians to

Live victoriously,

Grow spiritually.